Frenchy

"I Wanted to Get Back at Hitler"

Tracy L. Shaler

iUniverse, Inc.
New York Bloomington

Frenchy
"I Wanted to Get Back at Hitler"

iUniverse books may be ordered through booksellers or by contacting:

iUniverse
1663 Liberty Drive
Bloomington, IN 47403
www.iuniverse.com
1-800-Authors (1-800-288-4677)

ISBN: 978-1-4401-1755-8 (pbk)
ISBN: 978-1-4401-1756-5 (ebk)

Printed in the United States of America

iUniverse rev. date: 3/3/2009

Dedicated to Holocaust Survivor
Jeannette Grunfeld Marx,
and in honor of her parents,
Salomon and Marianne Marx,
who loved her enough
to set her free on the Kindertransport.

"The Holocaust is a central event in many people's lives, but it also has become a metaphor for our century. There cannot be an end to speaking and writing about it. Besides, in Israel, everyone carries a biography deep inside him."

Aharon Appelfeld

CONTENTS

Frenchy

Foreword

When Tracy Shaler learned of Jeannette Grünfeld Marx's life story she was not only deeply moved by it, but also knew that her experiences had to be recorded and passed on to future generations. This book is unique in that it is not just a biographical account: the author, who is a detective by profession, meticulously researched all historical events related to this story, providing source material from Jeannette's personal collection, as well as numerous documents from German and English archives.

The story of a *Kindertransport* child is woven into the fabric of her family's history. It leads us from a past with deep and ancient roots in Germany to the Nazi Era, with its horrific eradication of all German Jewish life within a few short years. We also are given a rare glimpse into the inner workings of the London Auxiliary Ambulance Service during the War, where Jeannette Marx had joined up as a volunteer. Although an extremely important and heroic Service, not much was written about it in the past, and this account adds important information on this nearly forgotten Service.

Books and essays about the Holocaust tend to elicit strong reactions. Some readers greatly appreciate the information, while others feel that more than enough has been said about this topic, and that it should best be put to rest. When conversing with younger Germans I was repeatedly asked why they should have to deal with the sins of their parents or grandparents.

Since the actions of individuals contribute to historic events, and history tends to repeat, our efforts should be directed at learning from past mistakes and evils, and to make sure we don't repeat them. Many seem to think that the Holocaust was a mere aberration, a tragedy that could not possibly happen again in the Western world. However, one should keep in mind that this evil murder machinery was instituted only 60 to 70 years ago by a cultured and educated people who took great pride in their Christian roots and morals. After transcribing and translating many original documents from the Nazi Era, I have come to the conclusion that most everyone in Germany knew that Jews were degraded, mistreated, robbed, and murdered. Once the Law on name changes was introduced on 17 August 1938 [§ 2 of Ordinance 2], as well as other laws restricting the lives of Jews, every village mayor, registrar, municipal clerk, and police officer joined this government-sanctioned effort. There was no public outcry or concerted effort denouncing these laws. After implementation of Regulation 11 of the Civil Code of the Reich from November 28, 1941 (RGBI. I S. 722 ff.), accountants, as well as tax office- and bank employees were well aware that Jews were being stripped of all their assets. Numerous deportation orders were sent by mail, passing through the hands of postal employees. Many railway officials, railway workers, auctioneers, landlords, neighbors, journalists, school teachers, and soldiers knew exactly what was going on. But the majority of citizens either chose to willingly cooperate with the Law, or to quietly stand by, so their own person, or family, would not be endangered. Every human being is responsible for his or her own actions, no matter what the political regime, and true humanity requires that we don't avert our eyes when murder is perpetrated, but do whatever is in our power to save the victim. Every man, woman, and child on this earth has to understand that differences in race and religion provide no license to kill, and that every human being deserves to be treated with dignity. That is one of many lessons of the Holocaust and of this book, a message that should be repeated over and over, until all of mankind can understand.

Esther Bauer, PhD

Preface

The story you are about to read is the true life account of Holocaust survivor Jeannette Grunfeld Marx. Although numerous books have been written about the Holocaust, no two stories are the same. Every individual has his or her own story to tell. The events described herein are the actual events Jeannette experienced as told in her own words. As time passes, however, memories fade and where the names of certain individuals could not be recalled, a substitute was provided and an asterisk placed next to it. For obvious reasons, events that occurred in her absence, (e.g., her parents' wedding) are recounted based on information regarding how Jews generally conducted their lives in Germany during this time period. Jeannette's story is set within the background and context of the significant historical events taking place within Germany and England at the time. Where appropriate, personal documents, letters, and photographs are included to enhance the reader's understanding of Jeannette's life under The Third Reich and during World War II.

We shall never forget.

A Nazi flag flies in front of the Cologne Cathedral, 1937

1

Roots Run Deep

Cologne, the high-spirited German city known for its glorious cathedral *Kölner Dom* and scented water, *eau de Cologne*, is also the city where Jeannette *Hanni* Marx celebrated *Karneval* as a child and received her first kiss as a young lady. Located along the Rhine, the city's inhabitants enjoy their local *Kölsch* breweries and restaurants as well as their wine, and maintain their contagious sense of humor. This is the place where laughter abounds and local culture and customs are cherished. Walking along the street in the heart of Cologne one might step into a nearby pub and order up a cool and frothy Kölsch brewed right onsite. There in the pub as you sip your fresh ale you might overhear, but not understand, a few jokes told in the local Kölsch dialect. It is difficult to imagine that not so long ago this city was also the very place where a Jew lay in silence, hiding within the darkness of an obscure cellar, as Nazis roamed the streets above like wild beasts on a hunt for their prey. This frightened and lonely victim scrawled these words on the cellar wall:

I believe in the sun, even when it is not shining.
I believe in love, even when feeling it not.
I believe in God, even when He is silent. [1]

Eighty-seven-year-old Jeannette Grunfeld, *née* Marx, has occasionally wondered if this person was someone she knew. Was he or she an acquaintance perhaps, or even a friend? What if this victim was one of her many relatives who stayed behind in Germany after she left? She will never know the answer to this question but she does know that she was one of the fortunate German Jews residing in Cologne during the Nazi regime. She knows, because she survived. For Jeannette, Cologne will forever remain in her heart as the home she adored, then detested, and, finally, reconciled with.

Jeannette, nicknamed *Hanni* at birth, is a petite, well-groomed elderly woman with silvery, short wavy hair. She wears glasses and a touch of red lipstick. Jeannette has an authentically warm smile, eyes that shine, and a laugh that is far from forgettable. What is it that she wants? More accurately, what is it that she does *not* want? The answer quite simply is that she does not want to be forgotten. Without hesitation and in a very unique dialectic mixture of German, British, and Bronx, Jeannette begins to tell her story.

"We came over with the Roman Legions," she says to emphasize the antiquity of Jewish presence in Germany. Jeannette was born in Cologne, Germany, on June 4, 1921, and her own rich German Jewish ancestry in this city stretches as far back as possibly the sixth to eighth centuries, as she was told by her mother, Marianne. The Romans initially settled Cologne in 38 B.C. and it appears that as early as AD 50 a number of Jews came along with the Legions. In AD 321, after dispersion of the Jews from Judea[(2)], Emperor Constantine referred to the Jewish community in Cologne in a decree issued to the Roman magistrate of Cologne containing instructions regarding relations with a local rabbi[(3)]. Early historical records also indicate that Jews lived in the "territories of the Frankish kings and worked as merchants, land owners, customs officials, doctors and master coiners."[(4)] The history of Jews in Cologne echoes the fate of Jews elsewhere in Europe, a people whose story is an interwoven tapestry alternately filled with tears of sorrow and tears of joy; oppression and freedom; murder and persecution; and exuberant life. When discussing the history of Jews in general, Jeannette questions out loud, "If we're God's chosen ones, why do we have to suffer so much?"

One example of shocking persecution of the Jews in Cologne occurred in 1096 when a man known as "Peter the Hermit" preached in a church on the site where the Cologne Cathedral stands today. The congregants listened intently to the Good Friday sermon. Peter blamed the Jews for Jesus' death, and concluded it was the Jews who should "pay." In a fury, the congregants rushed the streets of Cologne and rounded up as many unsuspecting Jews as they could find. Although the Archbishop tried to protect the Jews, many of them were murdered that day. Three hundred Jews were surrounded and given an ultimatum: be baptized or die. The group chose five men among them "to slay the rest."[(5)]

In 1431, the City Council of Cologne sent a letter to the Emperor justifying its expulsion of the Jews. Only 11 tax-paying Jewish families remained after the order went into effect.[(6)] Because of numerous persecutions, life was so volatile that by the fifteenth and sixteenth centuries Jewish numbers throughout the region had dropped dramatically.[(7)] Of the surviving Jews, most lived in abject poverty and insecurity. They faced periods of harsh treatment; then relative acceptance, persecution, exploitation; then invitations to live in peace again. But for German Jews, peace was always short-lived. Jews were subjected to restrictive Jew Laws, and required to pay high taxes.[(8)] In the cities they usually lived in the Jewish quarter, some of which were walled Ghettos with gates that were locked by the city's authorities at night. German Jews spoke Yiddish, a mix of medieval German and Hebrew words and phrases.

Jeannette's maternal grandfather, Josef Seligmann, was fortunate because he proved successful in business. A wealthy merchant from Cologne, he gave generously of his time and finances by co-founding the Orthodox synagogue at the *Glockengasse Synagogue*. Jeannette recalls attending there with her parents regularly throughout her childhood. Because of her grandfather Josef's contributions, his family members had their own reserved seating. Josef Seligmann was married to Jeannette Kahn, a relative of the famous Rothschild family from Frankfurt. The Rothschilds were known for their successful business and banking enterprises. Josef and Jeannette resided in a spacious apartment in Cologne decorated with fine furniture, oriental rugs, and eloquent works of art. The couple had seven children: Hedwig, Arthur, Sigmund, Bertha, Julius, Otto, and Marianne, the youngest, who was born at 5:00 a.m. on July 7, 1889. Marianne was Jeannette's mother.

Jeannette's paternal ancestors, on the other hand, came from small towns and villages. Her father grew up in Weilerswist in the district of

Euskirchen in North Rhine-Westphalia, approximately 20 kilometers southwest of Cologne. It is a small, picturesque community in the Eifel hills and home to the magnificent Water Castle *Kühlseggen,* which dates back to the fifteenth and sixteenth centuries.[(9)] Weilerswist is surrounded by grand forests, lakes, and other villages scattered throughout the countryside. In 1698, Jewish residents were documented in Weilerswist for the first time and by 1774 four Jewish families had made their homes there.

Dieter Peters, in his work *Land Between Rhine and Maas,* describes what life was like for these Jewish villagers:

> Jews in the Rhineland can be traced back as far as the Roman Era. There is documentation of the existence of a Jewish community in Cologne in 321. The Emperor pledged to protect the rights and property of Jews. With the decline of the Emperor's power rights were transferred to landowners. Jewish rights were confirmed through letters of protection connected with payments to the ruler. Jews were only permitted to settle in predetermined residences and to conduct business if they had such a letter of protection.
>
> Numerous ordinances were implemented for Jews, restricting their lives considerably. They were not permitted to buy property, and were mostly required to make a living through lending. In the 18th Century Jews were permitted to become butchers or peddlers, and they could also buy houses, but most of the Jews in the area of our village were poor.
>
> In 1791 civil rights were extended to Jews in revolutionary France, and when our area was occupied (1794) French law was implemented, and Jews became free citizens. In 1808 Jews were forbidden by the French administration to peddle, and therewith an important means of income had been lost. In this ordinance Jews were also required to accept a fixed surname, and thus ended the tradition of using the father's given name as part of the surname. In 1815 the Weilerswist region became part of the Kingdom of Prussia, and laws prohibiting Jews from holding professional positions were done away with on July 23, 1847. Jews, however, were still prevented from being officers or teachers and did not have the right to vote.[(10)]

The name change ordinance required all Jewish subjects to relinquish their Hebrew surnames and adopt German names instead. Only those who already had "acceptable" surnames were permitted to carry on their old family name, but even some of those families changed their surnames at the time. Jeannette's great-great-great-great grandfather's name is recorded in German documents as Andreas Cain[2]. His sons adopted the last name of *Marx*, an approved German-sounding surname. Marriage records indicate that their mother, Sibilla, married one Adolph Marx sometime after the death of her husband Andreas. Her children may have been compelled to adopt their step-father's surname because it fit the requirements of the name-change ordinance. One of these sons was Michael Marx, Jeannette's great-great-great grandfather. Michael was born in 1790 in the hamlet of Metternich, which belonged to the municipality of Weilerswist. His brother, Philipp Marx, founded a synagogue in 1848. In 1869 the Jewish population rose to 54. The synagogue of Weilerswist belonged to the Jewish community of the Euskerchin district. Jews united together into a "synagogue community" and Metternich, Vernich, and Weilerswist were a part of this community. In 1869 citizenship rights also included the Jews. Then, and for over 60 years, the government did not interfere with Jewish life.[(11)] Jewish children in these villages received a basic Jewish education by Jewish teachers hired by the community, however, by the second half of the 1800s they were required to attend German public elementary school.[(12)]

Michael Marx' son Hermann was born in 1825 in Kleinvernich, another hamlet belonging to the municipality of Weilerswist, home to yet another beautiful Water Castle, *Gützgensburg*. Hermann married Hannchen Wolf and had a son, Michael, Jeannette's paternal grandfather. Interestingly, historical records indicate that Michael had plans to immigrate to America in 1874, where one of his uncles was already living. Weilerswist archives contain old letters, wherein Hermann Marx requested permission for his 17-year-old son to leave, explaining that he was planning to emigrate for reasons of financial betterment, and definitely not to escape a possible enlistment in the army. Permission was granted to Michael, who at that time was described as a "butcher's helper," but for reasons unknown he never left. Michael met and married a Bavarian girl named Franzisca *Fannie* Nussbaum, and the couple settled in Kleinvernich next to his relatives. The oldest son of Michael and Fannie Marx was Friedrich Salomon Marx. He was born on July 23, 1888, and was Jeannette's father. Like Jeannette's grandfather, Michael Marx, many Jews in the western and southern parts of Germany were cattle dealers. In these towns, relationships with Christian neighbors in the 1800s were mostly friendly and neighborly. Jews spoke in the local dialect, and Christian and Jewish children grew up together, playing and running along the hills and lakes or venturing into the nearby forests.

In 1900, when Salomon, nicknamed *Sally*, was about 12 years old, he attended his cousin Hermann Scheuer's wedding. Hermann's bride to-be was Bertha Seligmann, 11-year-old Marianne's sister. It was here that Salomon first met Marianne, or *Jenny* as they called her. This dark haired city girl with the lovely brown eyes also had a great sense of humor, a trait that did not go unnoticed by her new friend Salomon. From this point on the two youngsters would visit each other at mutual family get-togethers and a long friendship ensued. Although Marianne lived in Cologne, she would travel to Weilerswist regularly to visit her sister Bertha, who settled there after her marriage to Hermann, a cattle dealer.

The year following Bertha's wedding to Hermann, Marianne and Bertha's mother, Jeannette, suffered a heart attack and passed away. After giving it much thought, Josef, who by this time was not in the best of health himself, thought it best to send his daughter Marianne to a boarding school in Switzerland where she could receive an excellent education. While there, Marianne learned to speak English and French. As part of her formal training, Marianne also acquired musical skills in classical voice and piano; she was known for her beautiful operatic voice and great passion for playing the piano. Life in Switzerland was going along well for Marianne until she received the terrible news that her ailing father had passed away. She immediately returned home to live with her two older brothers. Because she was the youngest girl in her family, Marianne's brothers were now responsible for taking care of her.

World War I

Marianne's friend Salomon Marx had grown up to become a self-confident and straight-forward young man who was known for his integrity and friendliness. He had obtained a very good education and graduated with a degree in business. When World War I broke out in 1914, Jewish associations encouraged Jewish men to volunteer for the Kaiser's army, as they believed this would help prove their loyalty to the Fatherland, and 100,000 Jews readily did enlist—a total of 17% of all German Jews between 17 and 45 years of age.[(13)] Salomon reported for military duty along with four of Marianne's brothers. All of them were foot soldiers stationed on the Eastern front, in Russia. The conditions of trench warfare were deplorable, to say the least. Soldiers had to constantly fend off the giant rats that took shelter in their trenches as artillery fire blasted them. What's worse, the vermin would constantly gnaw on anything made from leather they could find. Another ever-present and disgusting problem was that of lice. Oftentimes, the soldier would just have to pick them off individually to kill them. [(14)] When speaking of his war experience, a German sergeant recounted, "We marched on and on. We never dared take off our boots, because our feet were so swollen that we didn't think it would be possible to put them on again. In one small village the mayor came and asked our company commanders not to allow us to cut off the hands of children. These were atrocity stories he had heard about us."[(15)]

On the Eastern front, where Salomon and Marianne's brothers were stationed, German-Jewish soldiers encountered Eastern Jewish communities for the first time. What struck these soldiers so bluntly was the abject poverty the Eastern Jews lived in. By this time in Germany, most Jews were either middle class or intellectuals and had not experienced the impoverishment they were now witnessing. Ironically, what the soldiers also observed was that these communities possessed a true and deep faith, an optimistic outlook on life, and a "wise sense of humor." Because of this encounter, many German Jewish soldiers returned to practicing Judaism.[(16)]

There were only ten divisions of the German Eighth Army along the Eastern front, as the majority of soldiers were stationed along the

Western front against France and Britain. Those left on the Eastern front had to endure a major Russian assault and were outnumbered two to one. German soldier Paul Von Hindenburg, who would later lead the revolutionary Weimar Republic, was made Commander-in-Chief. Thanks to his shrewd military tactics, the German army was able to surround and defeat the Russian Second Army. Numerous soldiers from the Eastern front were then transferred to the Western front, but the American military had by then joined the war and the Allies were beginning to regroup. Although the Germans fought valiantly until the very end, the Kaiser capitulated on November 9, 1918.(17) Approximately 1.6 million German soldiers were killed, 4,065,000 were injured, and 103,000 were missing.(18) Of the 100,000 German Jews who fought, 12,000 gave their lives for the Fatherland and 1500 received the Iron Cross First Class. Salomon proved himself to be a brave and reliable frontline soldier and he was one of those recipients.

Salomon, along with Marianne's brothers were among the fortunate men who returned—but not unscathed. Two of her brothers, Julius and Sigmund, were injured: Julius was gassed and eventually died as a result of the debilitating effects of mustard gas. Julius, Sigmund, Arthur, Otto, and Salomon risked their lives voluntarily for their country and were now World War I Veterans. Leaving life on the battlefield behind and returning to business as usual at home must have taken some period of adjustment for many German soldiers. Unfortunately, some of them did not make the transition, especially in the face of defeat. Their bitterness festered into blame and vengeance. Among those soldiers was Corporal Adolf Hitler, a dispatch runner who had taken messages back and forth between the command and the battlefields during the war.(19)

After Germany's defeat and the Kaiser's flight, the new Weimar Republic was established and several prominent Jews participated in leadership roles. This did not bode well for many Germans, who began looking for scapegoats for losing the war and amidst a brewing economic crisis. German historian Hans Delbrück commented, "Germany is governed as little by 'the proletarians' and 'the Jews' as it was previously by 'the Junkers' and 'the student fraternities.' … After all, it is not so unnatural that it should be the Jews, in particular, who, after being shoved into a corner for so long, have now emerged into the front rank. But there are already signs of the backlash. Day by day anti-Semitism is gathering force." In Cologne on December 13, 1918, the *Israelitische Gemeindeblatt* wrote, "There is a scent of pogrom in the Berlin air" ... but the only Jews being attacked are those who do not defend themselves. Only Jews who have no respect for their own Jewish ness are despised. But we intend to cling to our Jewish ness to our last drop of blood."[20] Meanwhile, in Munich an obscure little group calling themselves the German Workers Party expressed their distain towards the Weimar Republic and put the blame on the Jews. Corporal Adolf Hitler, a new member, quickly moved up to a leadership role as he agitated other members with his fiery rhetoric and activist personality. Hitler later renamed the party the *National Socialist German Workers' Party*, abbreviated as the "Nazi" party. Given time, as the economy worsened and poverty soared, Nazi membership ballooned as well.

Undated photo of Josef Seligmann

Glockengasse Synagogue—1861

Euskirchen Synagogue founded by Philipp Marx[3]

2

Who Can Find a Good Wife? Her Price is Far Above Pearls

(Proverbs)

After World War I, Salomon took over his father's cattle business on the family ranch. Because of Salomon's honest and forthright transactions, his clientele base grew; his customers knew they could trust him. Salomon and Marianne had remained in contact over the years and their friendship blossomed into love. When the right moment presented itself, Salomon, who already received the blessing from Marianne's brothers, asked her to marry him. Marianne accepted, and plans for the ceremony were underway. The couple most likely would have had a *vort*, or engagement party hosted by a close friend or family member, and their evening would have been filled with laughter and celebration. As she was known to do, Marianne most likely would have told funny stories and jokes and perhaps even played a few pieces on the piano. Salomon was also known to have quite a sense of humor so he may have gotten in a few laughs of his own. In 1919, Salomon and Marianne were married in the *Glockengasse Synagogue* and, as is customary, Salomon would place the ring on Marianne's index finger and in Hebrew state, "Behold, by this ring you are consecrated to me as my wife according to the laws of Moses and Israel."(1) The ceremony would have then ended with Salomon shattering a glass, a symbolic moment reminding Jews of the Temple's destruction. The *seudat mitzvah*, or wedding feast, would have followed and included delectable entrees, dancing, and singing where the guests are commanded to help the newly wedded couple rejoice.(2)

Respecting Marianne's wishes to remain in Cologne, the couple chose a spacious apartment not far from where Marianne's beloved oldest sister, Hedwig, lived. A roomy, two-story dwelling, it was the perfect fit for the newlyweds. Some of the gifts the couple received were precious family heirlooms such as well-crafted furniture pieces, fine porcelain, and one-of-a-kind oil paintings passed down to them from earlier generations.

Salomon started a second business at the cattle market in Cologne selling livestock insurance. A nice addition to his career as a cattle dealer, the business proved successful because of Salomon's hard work ethic and integrity. The livestock business at the ranch was also thriving. Salomon had seven employees and traveled back and forth between Cologne and Kleinvernich to manage customer transactions. One customer of particular interest happened to be the British Army of Occupation. Army colonel J.H. Thorpe purchased horses on a regular basis for the military, and his business dealings with Salomon eventually led to a friendship. Salomon introduced the Colonel and Mrs. Thorpe to Marianne. Mrs. Thorpe was immediately impressed with Marianne's command of the English language and the two got along instantly. Marianne and Salomon extended invitations for the Colonel and Mrs. Thorpe to attend the opera with them—a cultural activity Marianne, along with most other affluent Germans, thoroughly enjoyed.

An outgoing couple both socially and culturally, Marianne and Salomon were surrounded by many diverse friends. They got along well with both neighbors and foreigners, and with family close by, Salomon and Marianne lived an extremely fulfilling life. Marianne's great love of music might be witnessed anytime, as she often practiced Beethoven sonatas or sang an eloquent score from a Verdi opera. The couple only lacked one special thing: a child to complete their happy union. That life-changing day finally arrived on June 4, 1921, when Salomon and Marianne welcomed their newborn daughter into their lives. They took her to the *Glockengasse Synagogue*, and when Salomon was called to the Torah, and after reciting special blessings and prayers, the family named her Jeannette after Marianne's mother. Jeannette's given nickname was *Hanni*, pronounced like "honey." Marianne's sister Hedwig and Salomon's sister Hanna visited regularly to assist their youngest sister in her new role as a mother.

3

"In my House, There was a lot of Laughter"

"Before Hitler, everyone was relaxed," Jeannette recalls. As she sorts through faded photograph after faded photograph she remembers, "In my house, there was a lot of laughter. I wasn't spoiled though; my parents were pretty strict but I was loved. They taught me to always tell the truth." Jeannette continues to recount her life, as she puts it, "*before* Hitler and *after* Hitler." As a child, little Hanni admired and deeply respected her mother. The two were inseparable; wherever Marianne went, she often took her daughter with her. Like the majority of women everywhere, Marianne enjoyed shopping. She browsed department stores and shops while walking along the cobblestone streets of Cologne. Marianne's favorite purchases, however, were the gifts she bought for others. On one such shopping excursion, she purchased a small, dark brown, leatherette *Poesie Album* for Jeannette. German children still use these unique albums filled with blank pages to give to friends and family so they can record their favorite sayings or poems. Most often, these endearments are written specifically to or for the owner of the album.

Jeannette cherished this special gift, and throughout her childhood asked several friends and family members to write entries for her. One of the more profound entries was written by her Hebrew instructor, Rabbi Reinhardt:

If I am not for myself,[4]

Who is for me?

If I am for myself,

Who am I?

If not now

When?

1931

Marianne and Jeannette spent many afternoons together window shopping, visiting the latest art exhibitions, or just taking leisurely walks in the park or botanical gardens. The city of Cologne had much to offer its citizens on a cultural level. Regarding German art and architecture, Jeannette was fascinated virtually every time she passed by the gloriously famous, gothic style, *Cologne Cathedral.* On a typical day out with her mother, Jeannette stood peering inside the window of a chocolate shop, admiring the colorful assortment of candies, cookies, and other confections. Suddenly, Marianne grabbed Jeannette and pushed her to the ground just inside the doorway of the shop. They heard male voices shouting obscenities at one another, then the sound of hurried footsteps stomping loudly over cobblestones. *Pop! Pop! Pop!* resounded through the air nearby as Marianne used her own body to shield her daughter. Jeannette could feel her mother's protective hands covering her head as well. Then there was silence. Shaken, Marianne slowly stood up and helped Jeannette to her feet, still scanning the street for any further signs of trouble. "I thought my mother was crazy when she did that. I didn't realize at the time that the Nazis and the Communists were fighting with each other," Jeannette recalled. Her mother explained to her what had just happened: a gun battle had erupted right there on the street in broad daylight. This was only a prelude to the events that were about to steal Jeannette's innocent view of the world as seen through the eyes of a child.

As startling and scary as the incident was, it did not dissuade Marianne from taking Jeannette to cultural events like the opera, where they watched performances such as "Hansel and Gretel." Like the majority of middle- to upper-middle-class Germans during the Weimar Republic, Marianne wanted her daughter to appreciate their refined German heritage. They often went to the cinema and various art museums such as the Museum of Applied Art, where locals could gaze at German textiles, finely crafted furniture, and rare jewelry. Meissen porcelain figurines were among the numerous exquisite displays there. Of course they also visited the *Historisches Museum der Stadt Köln* (Historical Museum of Cologne) where one could learn about Cologne's Roman origins. Also displayed was the *Kölnisch Wasser*, the original "Eau de Cologne" (4711) perfume that made the city famous. Marianne's favorite cologne, however, was *Channel No.5*. To this day, the world-famous scent reminds Jeannette of her mother, a woman who had fine taste in fashion as well. "My mother was polite, but she also spoke her mind. She had a terrific sense of humor and loved to tell jokes." Jeannette appreciated all of the qualities and gifts her mother possessed. Though kind and giving, she was also firm with Jeannette when necessary— a typical mom with great love for her only child.

Jeannette was also "daddy's little girl" and she remembers how well her father always dressed and that his suits were made by hand back then. Although Salomon worked many long hours, often traveling to Holland and Belgium, he always made time for little Hanni. The two took leisurely strolls through the city streets and Jeannette would sometimes bring along her little dachshund, *Lumpy*.

One morning Jeannette woke up with a temperature and a sore throat. Salomon came in to check on her. "What would help you feel better?" he asked. Jeannette managed to whisper a reply: "Coffee ice cream," she said, grinning slightly. Although it was a long distance, Salomon made the trip to the ice cream shop to pick up her favorite flavor. Salomon also knew how much Jeannette loved eating *ananas* (pineapple). They were quite expensive, but nevertheless Salomon liked to surprise his only child by bringing home a fresh juicy pineapple for a delectable treat. During the hot summer months when Italian families opened seasonal gelato shops in Cologne, Jeannette remembers accompanying the maid to retrieve a large bowl of icy cold, homemade gelato.

Salomon did not have a son, but that didn't dissuade him from taking his daughter to soccer matches or the bicycle races. The two laughed and carried on together as they cheered for their favorite team or cyclist. Admittedly, some of the favorite days Jeannette spent with her father were when he would take her to livestock shows so she could see all of the different animals, especially horses. The ranch in Kleinvernich was also a delight to visit because Jeannette, like most children, loved playing out in the fresh air, and besides, there were so many adventures awaiting a child's imagination in the countryside. Salomon employed seven Christian ranch hands and a maid, and every Christmas season he provided these employees with a Christmas tree and gave them all gifts to share with their families.

Salomon's kindness towards others was not reserved for only a special few. One particular evening he arrived home with a street beggar he had just befriended. Marianne welcomed the poor man into her home and immediately prepared a warm meal for him. Salomon went to his closet and retrieved some items to give to the destitute stranger. After tidying up, the grateful man thanked the family and disappeared into the night with a full stomach, dressed in new clothes, and with a pair of new shoes on his feet. Every Friday, Salomon faithfully placed an order for beef, then gave it to four impoverished families who lived in their neighborhood. One such grateful family was the Falkensteins. Mrs. Falkenstein was sick with tuberculosis, so, although Salomon did not himself eat pork, he brought bacon to her because at that time, bacon was considered medicinal for those suffering from tuberculosis. Salomon and Marianne's charity towards their neighbors was commonplace. Both of them gave time and resources to those in need, and also belonged to charitable organizations. Marianne was especially active in the local community, and the way she conducted her life bestowed honor on the Seligmann family name, which was well known throughout Cologne.

Hanna, or *Tante Hanna* as Jeannette referred to Salomon's sister, was very close to Jeannette and would soon play a vital role at a time when Jeannette needed her most. Because she had no children of her own, Jeannette was like a daughter to Tante Hanna. While living in Germany, "My Tante Hanna was a chef and owned a restaurant," Jeannette recounts. Jeannette was surrounded by excellent cooks, including her own mother. Ingredients can vary greatly from country to country, however, as Jeannette would unfortunately discover during a trip to France with her parents. "I ate Chinese food for the first time.

Well, I became very scared after I found out it was horse meat. I grew up with horses!"

Jeannette was raised in a relaxed, loving, and fun atmosphere. The Marx family invited friends and family over on Saturday nights, and while the men played cards and ate sandwiches, the women sat in the kitchen, nibbling pastries and gossiping over hot cups of freshly brewed coffee. Jeannette would giggle uncontrollably sometimes while eavesdropping from her room as the adults carried on with their funny stories and lively conversations. Marianne took great pleasure in treating her guests to her mouthwatering "continental cuisine," and Jeannette looked forward to these gatherings because of the delicious food that awaited her. She savored practically every plate her mother made. That is, except anything with spinach. And when she didn't want to eat it, her mother sent her to bed early. During family get-togethers when spinach was on the menu, she bribed her cousin Werner to eat her portion. Jeannette would slide her spinach over to Werner's plate and watch as he took each bite, contorting his face in disgust. She paid him to eat her spinach because she felt sorry for him. The joke was on Jeannette, however, when she found out later that he actually liked spinach.

Salomon and Marianne took Jeannette to Mainz, Germany, to visit relatives there who owned a brewery. As the family members gathered around the table to eat, the butler entered. Jeannette looked up, gasped, and raised her eyebrows. This butler, a large man with a frightfully serious look on his face, towered over the guests as he, in all seriousness, served each plate. Jeannette couldn't help but stare. Once the butler was finished serving, she watched as he took his place next to the service door, overlooking the table. When the butler caught Jeannette staring at him, she immediately looked down. *Oh no, what's this? I hate spinach!* Jeannette thought to herself. She looked back up at the butler, now staring directly at her. He raised a brow as if to ask, *Is there a problem?* Wasting no time, Jeannette immediately grabbed a fork then quickly and completely finished eating that dark green vegetable she so greatly detested, all while keeping her eye on the butler. When she finished, Jeannette glanced over at her mother, who by now could hardly contain her laughter. Marianne quickly realized who had encouraged her daughter to finally eat her spinach!

Marianne holding her baby daughter, Jeannette

1921

Jeannette and Marianne at the Botanical Gardens in Cologne, 1931

Undated photo of Salomon Marx

4

"My Father was a Cohen, and my Mother a Levite"

The Marx family, although not very religious, still observed the Sabbath and attended Orthodox services at the *Glockengasse Synagogue* on high holy days. Sometimes Jeannette would go by herself to the reformed synagogue, justifying this decision because, "The music was better and I liked the Rabbi." Salomon was held in high esteem within the Jewish community because of his lineage. Jeannette recounted, "My father was a Cohen, and Cohens are the first to be called to the Torah to read out loud and say the blessings. He also wasn't allowed to attend funerals … only for his relatives and that's it." Cohen lineages are traced to Aaron, the High Priest and brother of Moses, and to the tribe of Levi. Cohens are called to "exemplify the teachings of Aaron; to love and seek peace, love humanity and bring them to Torah."[(1)] One year, Salomon purchased a Torah with plans to start a Jewish community within their neighborhood. For unknown reasons, the idea did not quite come to fruition so Salomon decided to donate this Torah to the *Glockengasse Synagogue.*

Marianne played a significant role in the Jewish community as well. "My mother was a Levite and she belonged to a [Jewish burial society] who made vestments for the dead." An especially poignant moment for Jeannette came after Marianne's brother Julius died. Marianne helped take care of him for a long time after he had been gassed during World War I. Losing her brother was difficult since her parents were already deceased as well, and especially because Marianne's brothers Sigmund and Julius stayed home during this time to take care of her. They were so concerned about her well-being that they only married after Marianne was married to Salomon and they knew their baby sister would be provided for. After her brother died, Marianne sat *Shiv'ah,* the traditional period of mourning for seven days. "You sit on a low chair and say prayers," Jeannette explains. Watching her mother go through this painful period left a lasting impression on Jeannette.

Jewish holidays such as the *Pesach Seder*, or *Passover*, were a very special time for both the Marx and Seligmann families because the two would come together and celebrate at Salomon and Marianne's home. Once the celebrants broke the *Matzah*[5], they hid the *Afikomen* from the children, which is traditionally to keep them alert throughout the Seder meal. Jeannette recalls how this tradition of searching for the Afikomen was always her favorite. Once she and her cousins located it, each of them received a gift, "Usually chocolate, because we lived in Cologne, you know." After the wine was poured, Jeannette was asked to open the front door to welcome Elijah the prophet into their home. Frightened, she made her cousin Werner, not quite a year older than her, accompany her to the door. "I was afraid of the ghost," she recalls. Werner and Jeannette were very close as cousins and he wrote the following entry in Jeannette's *Poesie* album:

Koln-Nippes 4 March 34

Souvenir!

Learn to suffer without complaining

Learn to endure

And forbearance

Learn to forget and to forgive

Then you have learned to live

Written for you by

Your Cousin

Werner

Each Shabbat, Marianne lit a candle and cooked special food such as sweet bread, puff pastries, and chicken soup with short ribs. The family would then have dessert and "always a glass of wine because we come from the Rhinelands. Everyone had a wine cellar and my father knew his wine." A well-respected couple, Salomon and Marianne had numerous Jewish and Christian friends and acquaintances. Marianne had a particularly close friend, her "coffee sister," *Elisabeth**[6]. The two had known each other for several years because they were neighbors and visited each other regularly. They swapped recipes and chatted with each other in Kölsch over fresh bread and steamy hot chocolate or coffee. When either of the two was in need, the other would offer help at a moment's notice. Elisabeth's son *Karl** was about the same age as Jeannette and the two played together often. Each time Karl came over, he greeted Marianne and Salomon with, "Hello Tante, Hello Unkle!"

Like other children who lived in Cologne, Jeannette and Karl often asked their parents if they could go to the *Hänneschen* puppet theater. The puppets acted out silly stories and used local Rhineland humor as they told jokes to their young audience in Kölsch. No event was more anticipated, however, than the yearly celebration of *Karneval*. It starts in November and continues for three months, and local families help plan and then participate in the Mardi Gras-style festivities. Neighborhood groups get together beforehand for activities in preparation of "die tollen tage" which means, "the crazy days; three of them." There were jesters in the streets, parades, dancing, parties and many people donning *Kappens*, or fool's caps and masks. The delicious *Karneval* food, such as bratwursts, donuts, and savory potato fritters, were always crowd pleasers. The adults also celebrated after eating by quenching their thirst with a refreshing Kölsch.[(2)] Karneval was, and still is, a time of fun and celebration for young and old alike.

5

The Death of a Dream

As a student growing up in Germany before the Nazi regime came to power, Jeannette, although Jewish, attended a Catholic school. "In the neighborhood you lived in, when you went to public school it was either Catholic or Protestant." She attended the same Catholic school as her mother had when she was a child. Meanwhile, Jeannette's cousins attended the Protestant school located in their neighborhood. She continues to explain: "The first four years of public school was Catholic school. Then you have to pass a test and if you pass the test you went on to high school but you had to pay for it—it's private. Otherwise you have to go for eight years to public school, then you learn a trade." The priest at the Catholic school knew Hebrew and asked Jeannette to read to him what she learned in Hebrew class. "He says to me, what'd you learn in Hebrew school? So I had to tell him. Then he asked my mother can he take me to the church [Cologne Cathedral] and show it to me when he takes the other kids, and my mother says, 'sure, why not?' My mother said, 'I had the same experience,' cause his mother knew my mother very well cause she was born there, you know, in the neighborhood and everything. Can you imagine? Well, it didn't make any difference. See, where we lived there were not too many Jewish people anyway. Mostly it was my mother's family and some other families who had been there for years and years and years, you know. We had Christian friends; most of them were our neighbors and everything. I didn't know the difference. You were Jewish, you were a Protestant, or you were a Catholic, that's all. *Everyone was the same*."

Twice a week Jeannette also attended synagogue. As a Jewish student, it was customary for the boys and girls to attend school and additionally to learn Torah and Hebrew. Although her grades were not always perfect, Jeannette liked school and got along well with her classmates. "I wanted to be a doctor. We had a lot of dentists and doctors in the family and everything. Of course, my father's uncle was one of the first psychiatrists for children. He opened a school for children who were retarded to learn how to read and write and educate them. Nussbaum was his name." Dr. Nussbaum was the brother of Jeannette's paternal grandmother, Fannie. Jeannette had a cousin named Walter who was afflicted with Down's syndrome and he attended this school for special needs children. Although Walter was quite a few years older than her, Jeannette remembers that he successfully learned how to read and write. As a disabled Jew under Nazi racist and eugenic ideology, Walter would later become a target of torment in his own hometown of Weilerswist. Regarding other family members, Jeannette recalls, "They were either doctors or businessmen. They all had to have a doctorate or a college profession because [historically] German Jews were not allowed to have a trade. That's why they all went into professions. They had to be in business." For Jeannette, attending college was the logical next step. Once she completed her secondary education, she planned to enter medical school. After graduation, she would join the ranks of her other relatives by becoming a successful doctor.

6

"... Get Out!"

"This is a picture of Aunt Gudrun," Jeanette says while showing me a photo. "She was my Uncle Benno's wife and they never had any children. She was a famous German dancer and they weren't very friendly and, well, they had no kids, you know. Her parents were wonderful people; they were nicer to me than she was." Jeannette goes on to explain, "Her [Gudrun's] father was christened as a baby and he was a journalist for the Kaiser [Wilhelm II]. He purchased all of the gifts for the Kaiser. Both of his parents were Jewish but he never knew it until later." Jeannette knew Salomon's brother as *Benjamin*, although his given name was actually *Benedikt.* It is unknown why her uncle chose to go by Benjamin instead of Benedikt." Jeannette always referred to him simply as *Uncle Benno*. Benedikt Marx had a passion for politics and eventually entered the political scene in Germany. He lived in Berlin and was an elected member of the Social Democrat Party (SDP). The SDP represented the "interest of the industrial proletariat."(1) A highly intelligent and successful businessman, Benedikt was appointed to the Board of Directors of the Worker's Bank in Berlin in 1919. He was later voted into the Council of Economic Advisors of the Empire and, until 1933, he was the Executive Officer of the Nationwide Association of Bank Employees.(2) Benedikt met and eventually married Gudrun Hildebrandt, a well-known dance artist who performed regularly in theatrical productions, dancing to the music of Chopin in plays such as "Wolken und Wind." The couple enjoyed a bourgeois lifestyle, fraternizing with other well-known Germans in the trend-setting capital of Berlin. They had no inkling their lives were on the verge of grave disruption until September 14, 1930, when elections were held in Germany and the Nazi party won 107 seats in the Reichstag. Although the Social Democrats won 143 seats, Benedikt became astutely aware that Nazi ideology was clearly gaining popularity with the disillusioned masses.[(3)] On October 13, 1930, the Nazi party entered the Reichstag. The thunderous stomping of Nazi goose-stepping echoed through the building as the National Socialists marched in and role call was taken. Each Nazi party member defiantly shouted, "Heil Hitler!"[(4)]

Germany's recent defeat in the war, along with the suffocating war reparations imposed by the Treaty of Versailles, caused many in the German population to lose hope. The depressed economy and high unemployment rate only added to the grim mood of the country. The unstable situation served as an open door for the overexcited, highly emotional, leader of the Nazi party, Adolf Hitler. Coaching the volatile masses with a frenzied mixture of promises and lies, he riled them up. "Jews are our Misfortune!" became a national motto and Jews themselves became the national scapegoat. By 1932, over 13 million Germans (well over a third of the electorate—a substantial achievement in the Weimar electoral system) wanted a Hitler government. The radical demands for change and harsh discrimination against the Jews formed central elements of the Nazi platform, assuring them of extensive—though far from universal—support.[(5)]

> Amid the swirling mess in Berlin of political intrigue, rumors, and disorder, the SA, the Nazi storm troopers, stood out as an ominous presence. In the spring of 1932, many in the German democratic government came to believe the Brownshirts were about to take over by force.[(6)]

Benedikt was now completely convinced that if he didn't leave the country immediately, he would be killed. Fortunately, Benedikt and Gudrun had governmental contacts and friends in England and made immediate arrangements to escape there as soon as possible. Jeannette recalls the urgent phone call Uncle Benno placed to Salomon. "He told my father, 'Sell your business, take the money and get out!'" Benedikt did not mince words with this emphatic statement to his brother. "My father said to him, 'You're crazy, we've been here for hundreds and hundreds of years!'" Salomon, like many other Jewish Germans, didn't believe Hitler could maintain power over Germany. He would certainly be stopped before things got out of hand. As Jeannette recounts this decisive moment when her uncle practically ordered her father to flee the country, she explains, "We were born in Germany, 400 years in Germany! [My father thought,] 'Nothing will happen to us. I was in World War I.' He even belonged to the German Veteran's Association. We are Jews but we're German … but it didn't turn out that way."

Salomon's opinion regarding Hitler was, in fact, very much in line with what so many other Germans thought about him at that time:

> "Most of those, even within Germany, who thought they understood Hitler turned out not to understand him at all. Misjudging Hitler, underestimating him, misconstruing his aims, 'getting him wrong,' was commonplace. Many on the political Left thought he was little more than a sham and a charlatan, the puppet of big business, the brutal weapon of capitalism in terminal crisis, whose rule would be short-lived and collapse as capitalism collapsed. … The conservative Right tended to presume that, though he had his uses in whipping up emotions in the national cause, he was not much more than a mouthpiece of the disaffected masses, the demagogic leader of a protest party without a clear political programme, who, if properly 'boxed in,' could be contained and controlled until the 'traditional forces' of rule could re-establish themselves."(7)

Throughout Europe there were misconceptions about Hitler:

> But the immediate reaction of, for example, the *Daily Herald*, linked to the Labour Party and, with a circulation of over 2 million, the biggest-selling newspaper in Great Britain, was that Hitler was a "clown" who would soon fail to master the economic difficulties and the powerful vested interest he faced. Describing him as "a stubby little Austrian with a flabby handshake, shifty brown eyes, and a Charlie Chaplin moustache," the newspaper suggested that nothing "in the public career of little Adolf Hitler, highly-strung as a girl and vain as a matinee idol, indicates that he can escape the fate of his immediate predecessors" whose terms of office as Chancellors of Germany had lasted only a matter of weeks.(8)

Benedikt and Gudrun, under the real threat of death, fled Germany shortly before Hitler was made Chancellor and the Nazis took complete control of the Reichstag. Many other Social Democrats were not so fortunate. Those who stayed behind were either sent to concentration camps or assassinated.[9]

7

The Reichstag Burns

On February 22, 1933, at 9:14 p.m., an alarm sounded at Berlin fire station 9. Just days after Hitler was made Chancellor, the Reichstag was set ablaze. At 9:27 p.m., a tremendous explosion occurred and the great Chamber went up in flames.[1] It is unclear who set the fire, but Nazi propaganda conveniently blamed the Communists. Hitler rushed to the scene. His response: "The German people have been soft too long. Every Communist official must be shot. All Communist deputies must be hanged this very night. All friends of the Communists must be locked up. And that goes for the Social Democrats and the Reichsbanner as well!" Hitler left the fire and went right to the offices of his newspaper, the *Völkischer Beobachter*, to oversee its coverage of the fire. He stayed up all night with his propaganda leader, Joseph Goebbels, putting together a paper filled with tales of a Communist plot to violently seize power in Berlin.[2] As the Reichstag burned, Jeannette lay sleeping, unaware of what was happening. Salomon and Marianne listened to the news broadcast in shock and disbelief. The Reichstag incident set the stage for Hitler and his cohorts to begin unleashing their full fury of power and destruction. Philip Gavin, founder and author of *The History Place* website, observes:

> Hitler persuaded the aging President Paul von Hindenburg to establish a permanent state of emergency. This decree, known as the Reichstag Fire Decree, suspended the provisions of the German constitution that protected basic individual rights, including freedom of the press, freedom of speech, and freedom of assembly.

The decree also permitted increased state and police intervention into private life, allowing officials to censor mail, listen in on phone conversations, and search private homes without a warrant or need to show reasonable cause. Under the state of emergency established by the decree, the Nazi regime could arrest and detain people without cause and without limits on the length of incarceration. Hitler and the Nazi regime also resorted to simple and extra-legal terror to intimidate opponents. Nazi paramilitary formations, such as the Storm Detachments (Sturmabteilungen or SA, more commonly known as Storm Troopers) and the Protection Squads (Schutzstaffel or SS), had been established during the 1920s to terrorize political opponents and to protect Nazi leaders. After the Nazis came to power, many members of these units were recruited as auxiliary policemen and given license to arbitrarily beat or kill persons they deemed to be opponents. In addition, Nazi party faithful, in individual spontaneous acts of violence or in locally organized waves of persecution, assaulted those they perceived to be enemies of the regime.

The SS was a particularly important tool of Nazi terror. Its members staffed the concentration camps, in which perceived enemies of the regime were imprisoned. In addition, SS chief Heinrich Himmler also gained control over the regular (nonparty) police. Under Himmler and his deputy, Reinhard Heydrich, the SS centralized the German political police forces within a new agency, the Gestapo (Geheime Staatspolizei; secret state police). Together with a newly unified nationwide criminal police force, these plainclothes detectives used ruthless methods to identify and arrest political opponents and others who refused to conform to the policies of the Nazi regime.

In the months after Hitler took power, SA and Gestapo agents went from door to door looking for Hitler's enemies. They arrested Socialists, Communists, trade union leaders, and others who had spoken out against the Nazi party; some were murdered. By the summer of 1933, the Nazi party was the only legal political party in Germany. Nearly all organized opposition to the regime had been eliminated. Democracy was dead in Germany. Essential to the intimidating effects of the terror was the willingness of

> many German citizens (whether out of conviction, greed, envy, or vengeance) to denounce their fellow citizens, Jewish and non-Jewish, to the police. The Gestapo could not have exercised such control over German society without the benefit of this steady stream of denunciations, many of which were entirely unfounded. Many of the new Nazi authorities, including the SA, SS, and municipal administrative heads, established detention "camps" throughout Germany. In addition to actual camps, these detention facilities included old warehouses, abandoned factories, and other buildings. Here the Nazi authorities held political opponents without trial and under cruel and brutal conditions. On March 20, 1933, the SS established a camp in an abandoned munitions factory outside Dachau, located near Munich in southwestern Germany. The Dachau concentration camp would become the "model" for a vast system of SS-managed camps.[(3)]

Although it may have not been discussed out loud, Benedikt's words to his brother were prophetic:

> The new Reichstag met on March, 23, to vote the passing of the Enabling Act. In this session, all of the Communist deputies and 26 Socialist deputies were missing because they had been arrested or they fled the country. When the vote was taken, 441 deputies voted in favor of the Act and all of the Social Democrats present voted against it. Hitler now had dictatorial powers in Germany.[(4)]

Both Salomon and Marianne now knew beyond a doubt that Benedikt was right in regard to his own safety. If he had remained in Berlin, the Nazis would have arrested and killed him.

Now, having obtained dictatorial powers over Germany, Hitler focused his attention on what he would do about the Jews. "Perhaps," he told Goebbels on March 26, "the foreign Jews will think better of [boycotting German goods] when their racial comrades in Germany begin to get it in the neck."[(5)]

Jeannette does not recollect the events that transpired during the April 1, 1933, boycott, but Salomon and Marianne undoubtedly awoke to the following Cologne newspaper headline: "***Nieder mit Juda!*** (Down with Juda!). The announcement in the *Westdeutschen*

Beobachter, was entitled ***April 1933 – Boykott*** and urged Germans nationwide to boycott all Jewish businesses.

Each Sunday, Salomon conducted his business at the cattle market. Most likely, this Sunday would be no different, even after he read the morning's headline. Jeannette believes her father, based on his courage and principles, threw away the paper, retrieved his hat and coat, kissed Marianne goodbye, and cautiously but determinedly made his way to his insurance office located within the cattle market. He most likely carried on the day in a "business as usual" manner.

Contrary to their plan, the Nazi-orchestrated boycott had much less of an impact than expected. At this point, many non-Jewish, or *Aryan*, citizens had not yet ostracized their Jewish neighbors and some even defended Jewish business owners that day by intentionally shopping in their stores or conducting business with them. Acts of kindness that regular German citizens were showing towards Jews during times such as the boycott led many Jews to hope that the Nazis would soon be ousted. Like Salomon, a great majority of Jewish Germans were initially determined to stay in Germany and "wait it out," mistaking the variable kindness of their non-Jewish German friends and neighbors as a sign that the problem lay solely with this dictatorial government. The hope and false belief was that most Germans did not support the Third Reich and would eventually overthrow and abolish it.

Unfortunately, the Jews would soon learn otherwise. As time went on and Nazi propaganda was continuously presented in organized street marches, at the movie theaters, and over the radio, Jews became more and more ostracized. German businessmen now refused to fraternize with Jewish businessmen. German customers no longer frequented stores and shops owned by Jews. The most painful emotional losses, of course, were life-long friends and neighbors who stopped calling or visiting altogether. Many Germans aligned themselves with Nazi ideology and others just succumbed to fear. The Nazis made it clear that Aryans should not associate with Jews, and that if they did, consequences would follow.

The political climate in Germany was consistently worsening. Marianne, concerned for her housekeeper's safety, had to make the painful decision to dismiss her. It must have been especially difficult for

Marianne as this woman had lived with the Marx family for years. "My mom told our housekeeper, 'You need to go, I don't want you getting into trouble.' She was there for years. All the people that worked for us had been working for us for years. We used to invite them to see the Christmas trees and everything too." Jeannette remembers their laundress refused to relinquish her duties and would bravely travel to the Marx home in the middle of the night to avoid Nazi detection.

After the events of the boycott, the Reichstag, and the implementation of the *Enabling Act*, German Jews became more and more isolated. They feared writing letters, making phone calls, or even visiting one another.[(6)] German Jews knew they were no longer protected from any kind of abuse because the police were actually perpetrators, trolling the streets and watching every move that citizens made. Even a disgruntled citizen could beat a Jew before the approving eyes of the SS. German newspapers were also utterly worthless. They were chock full of nothing more than lies and propaganda issued by the Third Reich. Jews now turned to foreign media for their news and to each other for support and comfort in this time of darkness and rejection.

The Reichstag fire, Berlin, February 22, 1933

Westdeutscher Beobachter

Wochenend-Ausgabe
Samstag, 1 April 1933
Nr. 75 / Jahrgang 9
Preis 20 Pfg.

Nieder mit Juda!

Strafgericht über den Weltfeind bricht herein

Achtung!

Zur Abwehr

Der Weltpest an den Kragen!

8

"You're a Liar, Dr. Kreitz!"

In April 1933, the Nazis passed a new law referred to as the *Law for the Restoration of the Professional Civil Service.* This law forced Jewish teachers to leave the school system. They were replaced with Nazi instructors.[1] The Nazis had implemented a new curriculum called *Weltanschauung,* or *Worldview,* and now the public schools were referred to as *National Schools*. Instructors were told to join the *National Socialist Teachers Alliance* and subscribe to Nazi ideology, or risk being terminated. A classroom photograph from Holocaust archives depicts two young Jewish boys forced to stand in front of a blackboard. They are facing their classmates but stare at the ground as their teacher humiliates them. He is explaining what he has written in chalk right underneath his drawing of the Star of David: *"The Jews are our greatest enemy! Beware of Jews."*

The Nazi instructors got rid of many of the old textbooks and began teaching additional subject matter, such as eugenics and racial science. [2] This excerpt is taken from an actual guidebook for Nazi teachers called *The Jewish Question in Education* by Fritz Fink:

> The enormous significance of the Jewish Question is recognized today by nearly every member of the German people. This knowledge cost our people a long period of misery. To spare coming generations this misery, we want German teachers to plant the knowledge of the Jew deep in the hearts of our youth from their childhood on. No one among our people should or may grow up without learning the true depravity and danger of the Jew.[3]

Classrooms like Jeannette's now flew the Nazi flag and had a picture of Adolf Hitler hanging on the wall. Right before class began, instructors called the students to attention. The Nazi anthem, the *"Hörst Wessel"* would play and every student had to raise his or her arm in the Nazi salute.(4) Jeannette recalls that on one particular day, Dr. Kreitz,[*7] a self-proclaimed Nazi supporter, started railing against the Jews, spewing out vile propaganda to her captive audience of children. Jeannette grew furious and jumped up from behind her desk. "Well, I had a fight with the teacher. The teacher told me that all Jews are cowards, the Jews are this … Well, I went out of the school—I was only thirteen years old—pulled my father's decorations off the wall from World War I, the Iron Cross and everything from the War, and carried them back to school. I said, 'Here … you're a liar, Dr. Kreitz! Here's my father's decorations, my uncle was gassed, one was wounded … How can you say the Jews are cowards?' I showed it to everyone. There was another Jewish girl in my class and her father was even an attorney and she didn't say anything. And I was short and she was tall! I tell the truth because my parents taught me to tell the truth no matter what the cost." Because there was no such thing as free speech under the Hitler regime, the situation was not over for Jeannette. "Then the principal called me up. She called up my mother to come to the school. She says, 'Look, what you did was right, you did the right thing but don't say anything I told you because otherwise I lose my job. But you can't stay anymore.'" After this incident, Solomon and Marianne agreed Jeannette should attend a boarding school outside of Germany. They made arrangements for her to travel to France and attend school there.

Before leaving, Jeannette witnessed yet another terrible event that would tear away more of her childhood innocence. In an ominous foreshadowing of the horrors to come, on May 10, 1933, German university students gathered together and, while singing praises to Hitler, threw approximately 25 thousand books considered "Un-German" into raging bonfires all across the country. University of Cologne students had to postpone their meticulously-staged book burning ceremony because of rain. However, just one week later, on May 17, Jeannette watched in fearful disbelief as confiscated books by certain German, Communists, and Jewish authors and journalists were set aflame.[5] One consoling thought was that soon she would travel to France, a welcome reprieve from the inexplicable chaos in Germany.

As her studies in France continued for ten months, Jeannette grew extremely homesick and asked her parents if she could return. Salomon and Marianne deeply missed their only child so they gave her permission to return to Cologne. Jeannette immediately enrolled at the *Jüdisches Reformreal-Gymnasium mit Realschule*, a Jewish high school.

As Jewish oppression worsened, thousands of Jews were frantically trying to get their affairs in order so they could migrate to other countries. The director of Jeannette's high school called a meeting with the students, parents, and teachers to discuss the national crisis. The critical decision was made to teach all Jewish students a trade that would make them employable should the need to escape become absolute. "My parents had a meeting at the Jewish high school along with the other parents and teachers, and everyone and the teachers said we should get the kids together and teach them a trade too." Jeannette acquired the skill of dressmaking, and although she did not particularly enjoy it, she was very good at it. Like the majority of school girls her age, sewing was not the vocation she wanted to pursue as an adult. For Jeannette, attending college was the next logical step she planned to take after graduating from high school. But what was supposed to be within the realm of probability—Jeannette's dream of being a doctor—was rapidly diminishing. "The difference is like day and night. We had to learn Hebrew and the girls learned how to sew and the boys learned how to be carpenters or toolmakers. School was now from 8:00 a.m. until about 5:00 p.m."

One day as Jeannette was leaving school she was physically attacked. A group of males belonging to the Nazi Youth saw her and started to follow her. "I was coming from school; they pulled me off the bike [saying], 'You dirty Jew!' you know. Somebody knew me … a boy I went to school with before [had identified her as a Jew]. My knee was [hurt] so bad I was in bed for a month." Now no child was safe going to and from school. Young Jewish children were just as susceptible to verbal and physical abuse as were their teenaged brothers or sisters.

Although life now drastically changed for her, in many respects Jeannette was still a typical young teen. She enjoyed spending time with her friends *Mops* and *Jolly* as they compared notes on the latest fashions, listened to popular music, and gossiped about boys. Jeannette's first boyfriend was Rudi Billig, a dark-haired, brown-eyed boy who attended the same school as Jeannette. Jeannette's parents knew Rudi's parents and whenever he would walk her home, Marianne would invite him to stay and eat. The first kiss Jeannette ever received was from Rudi and they developed a close relationship. After all, they shared the same fears under the Nazi regime and the same hope that the nightmare would soon be over.

Going to the cinema became more and more difficult for teens during this time. Excerpts of speeches by Hitler and Josef Goebbels resounded throughout the cinema with disturbing images and anti-Semitic jargon. Nazi advertisements displayed torchlight processions and marches. The propaganda was relentless and virtually impossible to avoid.(6) One way Jeannette and other Jewish teens maintained some sort of semblance of normalcy was to join a Jewish youth group. One such group that Jeannette belonged to was comparable to the Girl Scouts. The girls would camp and bicycle from hostel to hostel until one day they were told they would no longer be accepted at the hostels because they were Jews.

Even the very special pastime of Cologne's *Karneval* could no longer be enjoyed by Jewish families because they were exposed to ridicule. A 1934 photograph taken in Cologne during *Karneval*, depicts a float with several German men standing on top of it. These men, mocking Jews who strictly follow Torah, are wearing black clothes and long fake beards and moustaches. For added insult and shock value, they are wearing large fake noses. The banner behind them reads, "The Last Ones are Moving Out."(7) Repugnant acts such as this one merely foreshadowed the nightmares to come. In 1935, the Nazis established what would be known as "The Nuremburg Laws." Jews were officially stripped of their citizenship.

> The first law, *The Law for the Protection of German Blood and German Honor*, prohibited marriages and extra-marital intercourse between "Jews" (the name was now officially used in place of "non-Aryans") and "Germans" and also the employment of "German" females under forty-five in Jewish households. The second law, *The*

> *Reich Citizenship Law*, stripped Jews of their German citizenship and introduced a new distinction between "Reich citizens" and "nationals."The Nuremberg Laws by their general nature formalized the unofficial and particular measures taken against Jews up to 1935.The Nazi leaders made a point of stressing the consistency of this legislation with the Party program which demanded that Jews should be deprived of their rights as citizens.[(8)]

By this time most of Jeannette's non-Jewish friends had abandoned their friendships with her. However, she had one special friend, "Luise," who refused to cower under Nazi pressure. In all likelihood, Marianne and Salomon expressed their concern for Luise's safety. After all, she was taking a great risk by coming to their home. Nevertheless, she continued coming to visit and proved herself a true friend when life for the Marx family grew even more dismal. At this point, teenage Jews were no longer allowed to even go to parks or swimming pools. Extracurricular activities for all Jews were systematically and permanently being stripped away from them, and their loneliness and isolation only intensified.

Jeannette's classroom photograph
Jawne, Judisches Reforreal gymnasium mit Realschule.
Jeannette is seated in the front row, third from the right.

Jeannette (seated second from right) learns to sew with other Jewish classmates

9

The Sting of Betrayal

On April 20, 1936, all over Germany ceremonies were being held in honor of Hitler's birthday. Most notable, however, was the fact that boys from 10 to 14 years old were being formally initiated into the Hitler Youth. Most likely, one of the boys in attendance that day was Jeannette's former playmate Karl. In order to become a permanent member of the Nazi Youth, Karl needed to pass a written exam regarding Nazi ideology and prove his race as an Arian. He would receive an *Ahnenpass*; a Nazi authority would confirm Karl's Arian bloodline, then sign and stamp the document. Karl also had to be in good physical condition, free from any inherited disease. Karl embraced the opportunity and made sure his parents understood the repercussions if they dared to try to stop him.[(1)] Eventually, laws were put into place stating that any parent trying to prevent his or her child from joining Hitler Youth could be imprisoned.[(2)]

Marianne received an unexpected call from her dear friend and neighbor Elisabeth. Jeannette remembers, "… and then we had always lots of friends and all of a sudden my mother's best friend called up. 'I can't come to the house anymore' she says 'Why?' 'My son, he is in Hitler Youth and he said, "Don't dare visit them, they're terrible people." He (Karl) called my mother 'aunt' and my father 'uncle' always! You know, when you're very close you called your friends aunt and uncle in those days—you didn't call them their first names, you know. He grew up in our house! I felt terrible because she was like my mother's sister, you know. We saw each other all the time. The kids were always over at our house too. He denounced his parents to Hitler Youth so they weren't allowed to have contact with us anymore." Marianne not only lost her best friend, but the news about Karl must have dealt her a major blow. This boy, who now denounced them, had always been treated like one of the family.

In addition to suffering the loss of personal relationships, Marianne was also forced to relinquish one of her most precious pastimes: the opera. Although not officially banned until 1938, the Third Reich made it virtually impossible for Jews to attend artistic venues. Due to the ever-present threat of bodily harm in the streets, Marianne stopped taking her daughter to concerts and plays.

The time came, too, when Marianne was no longer able to find solace through preparing comfort foods from her favorite recipes. As ingredients became more and more scarce, Jewish mothers found it difficult just to provide enough food for their families. "There started to be food restrictions [and we] no longer could go to the opera, or the doctor, or concerts, or cabaret—all that was all gone. Every afternoon the men used to go to the café but it all came to an end with restrictions," Jeannette recounts. She and her mother relished the art museum and now, that too was lost to them. Any art exhibitions that came to Cologne would soon be officially prohibited by the Nazis, although it made no difference because with no police protection in public life, most Jews no longer felt safe enough to venture out. Although home was the Marx family's refuge, the quiet chaos proved inescapable. Saturday night get-togethers with friends, wine, and fine foods were now non-existent, and Marianne, due to the internal fears now gripping her, would seldom sing or play the piano. Even the family's phonograph lay in silence. Jews were not even allowed to purchase records anymore.

The Marx family became more and more restricted to their apartment. The family regularly vacationed at a local spa where Marianne enjoyed reading works by *Goethe* or *Martin Buber* while relaxing in the sunny garden. Those restful days in a peaceful setting were officially over. *Bad Kissingen*, the only state spa left that continued allowing Jews to vacation there, eventually segregated them. Nazi supporters even held a rally and placed offensive signs in areas of the spa in order to upset and harass Jewish vacationers.[(3)] Salomon could not even take the family out to dine at a local restaurant; all of them now banned Jews. Jeannette's favorite aunt, Hanna, had already escaped to England at the prodding of Uncle Benno. Tante Paula and Tante Hedwig's families still lived nearby and Tante Rose also came to visit every so often. After all, Jewish extended families now relied more than ever on one another to keep each other from entering into complete and utter despair.

10

"I Was Hysterical"

Although Jeannette was in school when it happened, sometime in 1938 Jeannette's father was accosted by a group of Aryan men who demanded he relinquish his business to them. Unyielding in his resolve, Salomon adamantly refused. Furious at Salomon for his steadfast resistance, the group became enraged and overpowered him. They forcibly kidnapped Salomon and took him to an unknown location. There, they took turns ruthlessly beating him to the point of death. Meanwhile, Marianne was frantic the whole evening because Salomon had not returned home and she had no idea where he was. All she could do was wait for what must have seemed like an eternity to hear from him; after all, there were no police, no authorities she could call for help. Jeannette distinctly remembers, "They beat him so badly they paralyzed him. They brought him back the next day … they wanted his business. They wanted him to turn over his business to them. He said, 'Why should I? I started this business, I have it …' you know. We took him to the hospital after he came home. The money was no longer there. They took his business and his money. I didn't know a lot because my father kept a lot from me. I was hysterical when my father came home beat up." As Jeannette recounts this profoundly painful event in her life, she's unaware that she is slightly squinting; subconsciously trying to filter out the horrible images that remain in her mind, even after all of these years.

Jeannette does not believe the perpetrators were part of the "official" Nazi government such as the Gestapo, but she does refer to them as Nazis. Because Jews had no legal protection, any Aryan neighbor who wanted his or her Jewish neighbor's home, business, or material goods could confiscate them for a pittance or by force. Either way, the Jewish owner had no legal recourse to protect himself from exploitation. Although Salomon endured a horrific beating and survived it, within hours, the Nazis destroyed his livelihood along with any chance he had to escape Germany.

After her father was paralyzed, Jeannette says, "We still had the same relationship … he only said, 'I can't give you anymore what I used to be able to give you' … You know, it wasn't his fault. Well, we all made the best we could; we had no choice. We couldn't live like we used to live. They took everything away from us. Look, when they beat you up, you get paralyzed, you can't work anymore, they take your businesses away from you, what are you gonna do? You have no income." Jeannette remembers how physically and emotionally demanding the ensuing days became for her and her parents. Marianne was not strong enough to lift Salomon to bathe him, so some "Franciscan brothers" came to their home to assist the family. How is it that a decorated German World War I veteran who fought so valiantly and risked his life for the Fatherland, lay permanently paralyzed at the hands of fellow Germans? One German writer summed up this truth perfectly:

> The relationship between the German army and the Jewish-German soldiers of World War I is one of the most shameful chapters of German military history. The Jewish-German soldiers not only were abandoned by their former "comrades," but they were humiliated, abused and killed in concentration camps by former soldiers of World War I.[(1)]

Shortly after Hitler assumed the Chancellorship, the *Reich Association of Jewish War Veterans* Chairman Leo Löwenstein went so far as to provide Adolf Hitler with a copy of a memorial book documenting the names of 12 thousand Jewish soldiers who gave their lives for Germany during World War I. Supposedly, Chancellor Hitler acknowledged the book with "sincerest feeling," but soon afterwards all contact ceased and Hitler's office stopped accepting any further petitions.[(2)] The egregious assault on her father's life and the subsequent loss of income was incomprehensible. With Salomon's paralysis, any chance of escaping Germany now was all but lost. Where would they live and how would the family survive?

Thereafter, the family lost its apartment because they could no longer afford to live there. By now, the task of trying to locate a new residence was practically insurmountable for Jews. The pressure continued to weigh heavily on Marianne and she, in turn, relied heavily on the assistance of her relatives and Jewish community organizations now set up to help Jews in these tumultuous times. Jeannette and her parents could not escape the hellish nightmare they were forced to try and survive in. "We had to move to a small apartment then a different apartment. We kept having to move because we kept getting kicked out." It wouldn't be long until Jews were officially removed from the general population and relocated into "Jew houses" or overcrowded apartments with relatives or other Jews.[(3)] Jeannette's former classmate and Christian friend Luise remained faithful to the Marx family, risking her own safety to assist them. Marianne used the gold coins she was taught by her father to save and gave them to Luise for groceries. To avoid getting caught, Luise delivered the food in the middle of the night. Her service to them was invaluable and desperately needed because Marianne now had to physically care for her husband.

"Tante Hedwig owned a big apartment house and there was a butchery and grocery store inside the building. They were eventually forced to sell the butcher shop and the grocery store but they still owned their apartment." Jeannette and her parents moved in with Tante Hedwig on *55 Wilhelm Strasse.* They took all of their belongings and crammed into the tiny apartment room on the bottom floor. "She got an apartment on the first floor but the toilet was outside. Only two rooms you know … we used to have a library and everything in our home and we lost the house completely." The Nazis also stole Salomon's ranch and home in Kleinvernich. This was unspeakably painful as the property had been passed on to him by his father, Michael. Jeannette explains: "You have the house where you have the ranch and people working there. We slept there, you had a maid there, a housekeeper to cook and everything … for your family and for the help. We lost the house because they took it away."

Life continued to deteriorate as yet another degrading ordinance was passed on August 17, 1938, wherein all Jews had to accept the additional legal names of "Israel" for males and "Sara" for females. In this way they could easily be identified during random personal checks. Registrars added an annotation in the left margin of birth certificates. Friedrich Salomon Marx' 1888–1941 Birth Certificate contains the following annotation:

> Weilerswist, 31 October 1940
>
> According to § 2, implementation of the law to name changes dated 17 August 1938, person in opposite certificate has additionally adopted the given name "Israel."
>
> *Registrar's signature*[8]

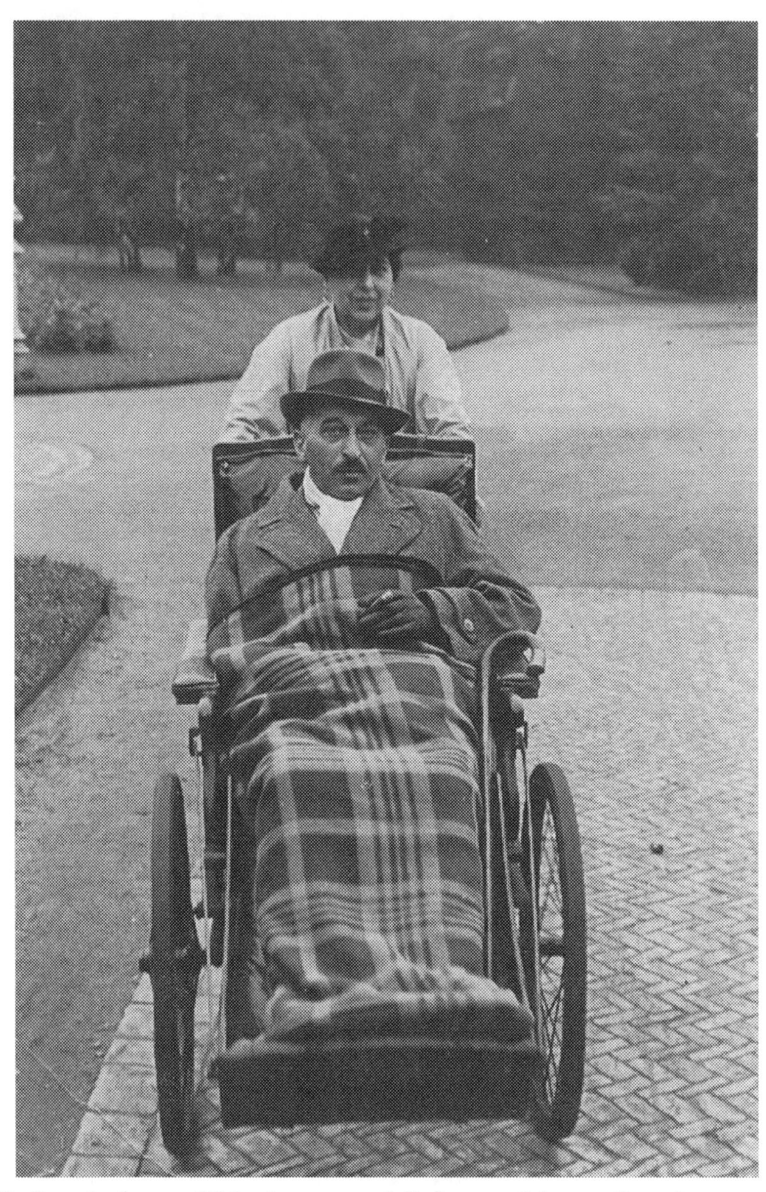

Undated photo of Marianne and Salomon Marx after the assault

11

Kristallnacht

Evening was approaching on November 9, 1938, when Marianne received a phone call from Elisabeth, whose son Karl had denounced them. "She told us, 'Go to the hospital!' She told us, 'They're gonna try and destroy everything Jewish, so go to the Jewish hospital, take Hanni with you, stay there and I'll let you know when it's safe.'" Marianne immediately readied the family and headed straight for the Jewish hospital. Shortly after receiving this warning, Nazi party members, including Hitler Youth such as Karl, took to the streets in a violent rampage against the Jews. Some local citizens even joined in on this hellish night of anti-Semitic brutality and torment. Hours later, German cities and villages nestled in the countryside lay in a heap of broken glass. This reprehensibly tragic night would soon be known to the rest of the world as *Kristallnacht,* or *Night of the Broken Glass.* Though portrayed as spontaneous outbursts of popular outrage, these pogroms were calculated acts of retaliation carried out by the SA, SS, and local Nazi party organizations.

> Hundreds of synagogues all over Germany, including Austria, were vandalized, looted, and destroyed. Many were set ablaze and firemen were instructed to let the synagogues burn but to prevent flames from spreading to nearby structures. The shop windows of an estimated 7,500 Jewish-owned commercial establishments were smashed and the wares within looted. Jewish cemeteries were desecrated. Mobs of SA men roamed the streets, attacking Jews and killing about 100 persons. In despair at the destruction

> of their homes, many Jews, including entire families, were driven to suicide. For the first time, Jews were arrested on a massive scale and transported to Nazi concentration camps. About 30,000 Jews were sent to Buchenwald, Dachau, and Sachsenhausen, where hundreds died within weeks of arrival. Release came only after the prisoners arranged to emigrate and agreed to transfer their property to "Aryans."(1)

Thanks to Elisabeth's forewarning, Marianne and Jeannette passed the evening with Salomon in the hospital, safe from the vicious storm that was raging outside. Thankfully, and for reasons unknown, this particular Jewish hospital did not come under attack. Jewish nursing homes, orphanages, and hospitals were invaded and ransacked throughout the evening. Absolutely nothing "Jewish," including their synagogues and cemeteries, were immune from destruction and desecration.

After remaining with Salomon in his hospital room for two days while the chaos raged outside, Marianne received word that it was now safe to leave. Elisabeth told Marianne that she overheard her son Karl talking to his friends about something "big" that was about to take place very soon. Deeply concerned for the Marx' safety, Elisabeth immediately contacted them. "We were able to stay in the hospital because of my father's paralysis. We stayed in the hospital until it was all over, then my high school was all burnt, the synagogues were burnt and everything and the businesses were all destroyed. The Jewish stores were smashed in … and they rampaged our house and they took stuff out." Although Jeannette's family escaped physical danger, they returned to their apartment only to discover that it, too, was vandalized and robbed. Jewish families were now unequivocally deprived of any hope that they might still encounter a little solace or safety inside their own home. In her book *Between Dignity and Despair*, Marion Kaplan describes the scene:

> A powerful image, mentioned often in Jewish women's memoirs, is that of flying feathers—feathers covering the internal space of the home, hallway and front yard or courtyard. As in Russian pogroms at the turn of the century, the mobs tore up feather blankets and pillows, shaking them into the rooms, out the windows, and down

the stairways. Jews were deprived of their bedding and the physical and psychological sense of well-being it represented. Broken glass in public and strewn feathers in private spelled the end of Jewish security in Germany.(2)

The *Glockengasse Synagogue*, the beloved synagogue Jeannette's grandfather Josef co-founded, was completely destroyed. Unknown to the Marx family, one item would be spared during this night of unleashed terror and destruction. As the synagogue burned there on Glockengasse Street, a German Catholic priest named Gustav Meinertz risked his life by running inside the fiery synagogue and rescuing the badly damaged Torah. He then hid it from the Nazis until after the war. The precious Torah was then returned to the Jewish community.(3)

The *Euskirchen Synagogue* located in Weilerswist and founded by Jeannette's relative Philipp Marx, was also ruthlessly destroyed. Almost seven years later, on September 1, 1945, an S.A. member and local Weilerswist villager would testify, without apparent remorse, as to his personal role in the destruction of the synagogue. *Note: Names have been redacted from original German document.*

Hearing:

Weilerswist, September 1st, 1945

Upon being summoned, there appeared the machinist— Weilerswist, 32 years old, and explained upon questioning:

I received orders from SA to appear at the restaurant at the Train Station in the evening of 10 November 1938. When I arrived already 30 to 40 men were assembled, several among them from other towns, whom I did not know. There I found out about the impending campaign against the Jews, and that synagogues in other towns had already been set on fire.

Since I live right next to the synagogue I became worried that my apartment might be affected if the latter would be set on fire. The people who had appeared were then divided into different groups for this campaign, and I noticed that most of us had been appointed to go to Heimersheim. But as no car arrived to pick us up we started in Weilerswist. I was ordered to go to the synagogue since I was the one who knew the location best. So I went home

> and got my wife and child out of bed. Meanwhile two SS men from Euskirchen drove up with their automobile. They had bought a canister along the way, in Massenberg, and now broke the door of the synagogue open and poured the contents of the gasoline can into the synagogue, along the side adjacent to the road.
>
> Using paper that had been formed into a ball, and which had been lit in my kitchen stove, the gasoline was set on fire. I was worried about my furniture, and also mentioned this. Thereupon the SS-man answered that I would receive new furniture from the State if there would be any damage. When the fire grew bigger, I walked to smith— by myself, who then called the fire department. They arrived soon, and kept moistening down my house so that it didn't ignite. The synagogue was a total loss, and I stood guard the entire night next to the fire. During this time the party member— Weilerswist came by at my place and called out to me: "In back you can buy cheap, there is enough stuff laying around there." My wife then retorted: "No, that is out of the question, my husband will stay here." I then remained next to the fire until around 5 AM, and then got ready to go to work. As I just remembered, towards midnight the SA-man walked by and shouted: "You cowards, why didn't you come along, we've had the high-life!"— was drunk. I deny to have been actively involved in the matter, or to have stolen anything from the Jews.(4)

Alfons Heck, a former member of Hitler Youth observed, "After Kristallnacht, no German old enough to walk could ever plead ignorance of the persecution of the Jews, and no Jews could harbor any delusion that Hitler wanted Germany anything but *judenrein*, clean of Jews."(5)

Germans pass by the broken shop window of a Jewish-owned business that was destroyed during Kristallnacht.

Photograph of the Glockengasse Synagogue immediately after the November 9, 1938, Pogrom

12

Kindertransport

The *Kindertransport Association* describes the events that followed the November pogrom:

> As soon as the world learned of Kristallnacht, efforts were underway to save Jewish children from the Nazis. The British Committee for the Jews of Germany and the Movement for the Care of Children from Germany persuaded the British government to allow Jewish children in Germany to take refuge in Britain. The Kindertransport was established. Between 1938 and 1940, approximately 10,000 Jewish children *under the age of 17* [emphasis added] were admitted on the Kindertransport. Immediately after the Nazis came to power in Germany in 1933, the persecution of the Jews began. Within months, tens of thousands of Jews left Germany. But soon emigration slowed considerably as visas became impossible to obtain. The ferocity of pre-war persecution of Jews reached its pinnacle with the pogrom of November 9 and 10, 1938, known as "Kristallnacht" [the night of broken glass], when German and Austrian Nazis burned and destroyed 267 synagogues, killed 100 people, smashed 7,500 Jewish stores [all that remained in the Reich] and incarcerated nearly 30,000 in concentration camps. Even after this, very few countries were willing to take in Jewish refugees. For this, the world at large bears guilt, the U.S. being one of the worst offenders. Until the start of World War II, when borders closed, Jews were allowed to leave (though they were not allowed to take out any possessions or money) and Jews trapped

> throughout the Reich struggled to find a country that would let them in. In response to the events of November 9 and 10, the British Jewish Refugee Committee appealed to members of Parliament and a debate was held in the House of Commons. It was agreed to admit to England an unspecified number of children up to age 17. A 50 Pound Sterling bond had to be posted for each child "to assure their ultimate resettlement." The children were to travel in sealed trains. The first transport left barely one month after Kristallnacht, the last, just two days before war broke out [September 3, 1939], which put an end to the program. Approximately 10,000 children made the trip. When the children arrived in England, some were taken in by foster families, some went to orphanages or group homes, and some worked on farms. They were distributed throughout Great Britain [England, Scotland, Wales, and Northern Ireland]. Once there, they were at no more risk than the rest of the population. This was not inconsiderable since many towns were heavily bombed. Mostly, the children were well-treated and grew up to develop close ties to their British hosts. A few were mistreated or abused. A number of the older children joined the British or Australian armed forces as soon as they reached 18, and joined the fight against the Nazis. Most of the children never saw their parents again. Of the 10,000, it is believed that 20–25% eventually made their way to the U.S. or Canada. It is from these that the Kindertransport Association of North America (KTA) draws its members. The last transport from Germany took place on September 30, 1939.[(1)]

Salomon and Marianne both knew that even if they could not leave, they had to get their daughter out of Germany as soon as possible. "So what happened was we went to the Jewish hospital and they destroyed everything. Then my father says, 'You have to get out where you don't come back anymore' cause he couldn't get out and my mother wouldn't leave him." Tante Hanna, now in England, "called to tell my family they're sending a transport to England so Hanni better get out." Jeannette's parents wanted desperately to get her on the Kindertransport but they had a major problem: Jeannette was 17-½ years old and had already missed the cutoff of 16. Salomon and Marianne were determined, however, to get their only child out of the country. They resolved to find a way. "My parents knew [about the age requirement]. I didn't know. My parents had connections in England, you know with my uncle there and my aunt worked with people who were also working with the people involved in the Kindertransport … she worked with very rich people. They arranged for me to come out and my parents had to pay double. But I made it. Isn't that something if you don't have connections you never can make it. They made sure I lived … that's what parents do for their kids."

Because of his paralysis, Salomon had no chance of escaping Hitler's regime. Countries that were willing to accept Jewish refugees wanted healthy individuals who were employable in specific areas. Marianne, however, spoke English and French and had other marketable skills such as cooking and would most likely have been able to secure her passage out of Germany. However, she refused to leave her husband behind. Marianne believed that her daughter, with help from friends and family already living in England, could make a way for herself. She knew Salomon needed her more. Her parents, of course, kept this hopeless fact to themselves and even reassured Jeannette: "You go now, and we'll join you soon." On the days leading up to her departure, Jeannette began bidding farewell to friends and family as is evident from entries made in her *Poesie* album at that time:

Her special friend Luise wrote this:

Cologne, January 3rd, 1939

Friendship!

A friend who is far away,

Of whom we know that he is happy,

Is very good company to us.

Oh, how everything looks clearer when distant,

While it confuses us while present!

Perhaps you will recognize, how surrounded by

Love

You were everywhere, and how valuable

The faithfulness of true friendship, and how

The world far and wide, does not replace

Those who are closest.

Dedicated in true friendship

Luise

Jeannette's best friend and classmate "Jolly" wrote:

Dear Hannes,

When you once as Grandmama

Sit in a recliner next to Grandpapa,

Remember often and cheerfully,

Your girl friend Jolly.

Don't forget me, I won't forget you either.

In eternal remembrance of your

Jolly **1 January 1939**

"Mops," Jeannette's other best friend and classmate wrote:

Dear Hannes,

Think of me often,

Just as I think of you

Back to the time before our apprenticeship

When we spent many a happy hour together,

Such hours I wish for you

During your distant path in life as well.

Your Pug **"Mops" 1 January 1939**

January 18, 1939, was a dark and bitter day for Jeannette and her parents.

The following quotations taken from *Between Dignity and Despair* captures the heartache well:

> For parents, the decision to send off a child was the most excruciating moment of their lives. The expression "children turned into letters" [aus Kindern wurden Briefe] revealed their despair.
>
> "The separation from my only child was heartbreaking. For many days and nights I lay in my bed, crying, and didn't want to live anymore."(2)

"It wasn't easy. Unfortunately, I wasn't able to take anything with me. I have nothing [photos] from my father's side of the family. We had a lot and we owned a lot of paintings and everything, but I couldn't take anything." Under Nazi regulations, Jews trying to flee Germany had to create a meticulous log listing every single item and amount. If they discovered a single error or discrepancy or any items in the suitcase did not match the log, they were confiscated at best, or the trip could be cancelled or postponed. At worst, one could be arrested. Marianne dutifully prepared a detailed list of every single item. Jeannette was permitted to take along only one suitcase, Marianne and Salomon shipped a trunk of items to her as well. Although extremely risky, Marianne gave Jeannette a few items she did not include on the required list. Marianne hid a gold coin wrapped in thread in Jeannette's sewing kit because, "Nobody looked at those things … And there was a diamond in there too," Jeannette recalls with a chuckle. The diamond was "a little one, a tiny one. She had bigger ones they took away … but at least you know … [she had gold] because her father told her, 'You have to have gold …' They didn't [suffer during] the Depression because they had enough gold. They always kept it hidden, you know … under the floor." The gold coins Marianne kept hidden were what sustained the family during the Nazi persecution.

When the Third Reich issued "new" birth certificates to all Jews, they were forced to appear in person and "apply" for the newly issued certificates now containing the added names of *Sara* or *Israel.* Jeannette carried her new birth certificate along with her other necessary documents. "My parents, they took a cab. My father couldn't drive me. They didn't have nothing anymore; they lost a lot of things. They weren't allowed to come upstairs when we were leaving because somebody, when they couldn't say goodbye to the kids, took her out of the window and he took her home with him again … before I left, you know." Jeannette was referring to a situation that had occurred involving a father who could not bear the final goodbye at the train station. Crying, he reached inside the train window and pulled his only daughter right back through and took her home. Both of them would later be deported to a concentration camp. Of course, Jeannette was a teenager by now and was too big to fit through a window, but the rules still applied to everyone.

Jeannette hoped that she would see her parents again and they told her, "When everything is over, you'll come back." Jeannette stated she didn't know there would be a war after she left. Her mother tried telling her different things to reassure her frightened daughter. "You have to go." "We'll try and come." "They'll [Benedikt and other relatives] get us out." Jeannette recalls, "But she was lying to me." Jeannette was about to board the train when her mother, not wanting her daughter to fall into the trap of self-pity, looked into her eyes and reminded her once again, "Someone always has a bigger package to carry than you." Marianne, as strong as she was, could not hold back the tears now as she and Salomon hugged and kissed their only daughter goodbye. "I love you very much and I will never forget you," were the last words Jeannette said to her devastated parents. "What are you gonna do? You can't do nothing about it. Thank God my parents loved me enough to let me go, you know. Every parent knew that when they said goodbye to their kids, they felt that they wouldn't see them anymore. I was very fortunate not to be in a camp but I survived. I went with the children's transport, I was on my own, which is not easy when you're a spoiled brat. Thank God I wasn't that spoiled." Jeannette climbed the stairs alone, checking back as she neared the top to get one last look at her parents and her life in Germany, and she gave them both a final wave goodbye.

Included in the list Marianne prepared for the Kindertransport is her "Poesie" album[9]

Salomon, Marianne, and Hanni in a photograph taken before she left on the Kindertransport

6469

H.O. 2143

E1

Geburtsurkunde

(Standesamt K ö l n - Nippes Nr. 544)

Jeanette M a r x

ist am 4. Juni 1921

in K ö l n - Nippes geboren.

Vater: Friedrich Salomon Marx, Viehhändler,

Mutter: Marianna Seligmann

Änderungen der Eintragung Das nebenbezeichnete Kind Jeanette Marx führt auf Grund der Verordnung vom 17.8.1938 zusätzlich den Vornamen "Sara"

K ö l n - Nippes, den 7. Januar 1939.

Der Standesbeamte

In Vertretung

(Siegel)

Gebühren .-60 RM

No. 279 des Gebühr.-Reg.

Copy of Jeannette's August 17, 1938, Nazi-issued birth certificate renaming her "Sara." Jeannette's name is misspelled "Jeanette."[10]

13

England's Open Arms

"I took 10 marks and a small suitcase. They collected all the kids and put us on a train. We were sent to Holland, stayed a couple of hours, then put back on a boat and I got as sick as a dog. I didn't realize really how bad it's going to be and at that age you still have hope but nobody else I knew was on the *Kindertransport.* A Dutch or English woman was in charge...I blocked everything out. We went by train to Holland and from Holland we went on the boat to England. I was helping with the kids … I was older than most of them so … I looked after a little girl." Jeannette had five years of French and she had briefly lived in France but she only had one year of English. Luckily, Marianne and her friends from England conversed in English frequently enough that Jeannette was exposed to the language to the point that she already understood and spoke it fairly well before her arrival in England.

Tante Hanna met Jeannette in London upon her arrival. She then took her to stay with a family who was related to an uncle on her father's side of the family. Tante Hanna, although she was a chef and owned her own restaurant in Germany, gratefully accepted a position as a maid in England. The pay was sufficient enough for her personal expenses but she had no way of supporting or sheltering Jeannette. "My aunt was only a housekeeper but she was good to me, you know." Not long after Jeannette arrived in England, she went to Hyde Park. Astonished, she listened attentively to English citizens as they freely conversed with one another regarding the political climate. At that moment, Jeannette realized, "No one was afraid of persecution or speaking out against the government." It was a stark reminder of the oppression she had left behind in Germany.

Jeannette goes on to explain. "So then I went to England and I stayed with people we knew, but they were very … They were horrible. They used to come to Germany to visit us and they were so nice." When Jeannette moved in with this same family who used to visit her family in Cologne, they changed towards her. "They were very nasty. It was winter, it was cold, and I didn't have nothing to cover. I used to take stuff out of my suitcase and cover up. They had kids my age and I shared a bedroom with the daughter; she wasn't happy about that and then, they weren't very nice. They didn't give me a blanket. I had thin blankets and it was winter." Jeannette recalls, "They were really cold and I was surprised because they were always, you know, when they came to visit us, we treated them royally, like you're supposed to treat friends."

Uncle Benno and Aunt Gudrun also lived in England but did not invite their niece to live with them and this always bothered her. "Even my uncle didn't offer me to come. He worked for the government. I don't know what he did, you know. My uncle never had kids. The two of them … forget it. I stayed with them a short time, a week while their maid was off and they complained I ate too much!" Gudrun even called Tante Hanna to complain. Of course, Hanna defended Jeannette: "What do you expect? The poor girl was hungry!" Aunt Gudrun was not very friendly, but her father, Mr. Hildebrandt, was kind. He led a privileged life working for the Kaiser until the Nazis came to power, and although he was a Christian and did not practice Judaism, he, too, had to flee Germany. Under new, Nazi-imposed, "racial laws" a person was Jewish "by blood" if either or both parents were Jewish. Some individuals and families registered and raised as Christians discovered to their dismay that by Nazi definition they were still Jews.. They, too, faced discrimination, but without Jewish organizations, friends, or relatives to console them. Nazi racial obsessions and laws were wreaking havoc with generations of assimilation.(1) Fortunately, Mr. Hildebrandt's son-in-law Benedikt provided the needed support.

Not long after Jeannette arrived in England, she found employment as a dressmaker on Bond Street. Jeannette met a girl where she worked who told her about a room that was for rent. Jeannette made enough money to cover room and board, but did not have much left over for food. "I ate lots of crackers and cheese and spaghetti and toast at night, or baked beans and toast. That's all I had for lunch every day. It was the cheapest." Jeannette's situation in her newly rented room proved short-lived, however. "Every time I wanted to get washed, the guy came in. The husband, so see I had to get out. Then I lived with an elderly lady and I didn't have to pay anything. Just that she had somebody to live with and help a little bit, you know. I went to work in September, then the War broke out."

A Jewish youth wearing a numbered tag sits on a staircase with her head in her hands after her arrival in England with the second Kindertransport.

14

"It is Evil Things We Shall be Fighting Against"

Prime Minister Neville Chamberlain

At 11:00 a.m. on September 3, 1939, British Prime Minister Neville Chamberlain announced, "This country is at war with Germany."(1) At 11:27 a.m. the air-raid sirens of London sounded. A stray French airplane had mistakenly entered British airspace and set off the false alarm. For many, "The first alert was terrifying."(2) After the air raid, Jeannette returned home as soon as possible. "When I came back home, my suitcase was with the doorman, that's because [the elderly woman's] son sent for her to take her to the country. She didn't leave me a penny. I mean, if you had a child … living with you … and she knew I had no money or anything. I went to work in the morning and I came home and they declared war. We didn't have bombings or anything yet. The war was declared and she left and I was there with a suitcase." Jeannette hurriedly called Tante Hanna on the phone and she promptly made arrangements for Jeannette to stay with some friends for a few days until she could find a more permanent living situation. Jeannette could no longer go to work now because of the War.

While staying with Tante Hanna's friends, she heard that a hostel had been opened for Jewish girls like her who had no money and were on their own. They interviewed her then gave her some money, which she gave back to her aunt to reimburse her for what she paid for Jeannette's previous living arrangements. Jeannette stayed at the hostel but worked under the table because, "I couldn't just sit there and do nothing." She paid the hostel a small rent. The hostel was in a nice neighborhood and it housed up to 25 girls. There were five girls to a room with one bathroom located in the middle of each floor. The other side of the hostel is where the younger children resided.

Everyday life had now drastically changed for London's citizens and Jeannette, still a teen, was right in the middle of it all. In preparation for war, trenches were dug in parks and other public spaces in case some people were caught outside. The greatest fear Londoners had was of getting gassed. Free gas masks were distributed, and children received "Mickey Mouse" gas masks.[(3)] ARP (Air Raid Precaution) organizations divided districts into approximately 10,000 people each and added several wardens' posts. The wardens were outfitted with yellow gas-proof oil skins, boots, and respirators. They were primarily middle-aged, middle-class individuals, both male and female, who served as "the frontline infantry."[(4)] Television programs went off the air and only one radio station was now available. Families stocked up on food while wardens passed through the city yelling, "Put out that light!" whenever there was the slightest light usage infraction.[(5)] One could not so much as light a cigarette—any source of light might aid the enemy in providing a target.

Jeannette missed her parents deeply and continued to wonder how they were doing. Although Jeannette had the familial support of Tante Hanna, she longed to see her mother and father. Jeannette felt virtually alone; a teenager now living in a foreign country with its own language and customs. Adding to the isolation was the uncertainty of what would happen now that her host country was at war with her homeland. Following are excerpts from cherished cards and letters sent to Jeannette by her family and friend Luise while they suffered daily under insurmountably cruel conditions. On the surface, the writers obviously do not want Jeannette to worry for them, but it is not hard to detect the dismal tones written "between the lines." [11] Keenly aware that their letters were subject to the scrutiny of Nazi eyes, it appears that her family, at times had to resort to the use of cryptic words and messages.

My dear Hanni!

Hopefully you received my letter to aunt [perhaps Hanna]. We received news from her, but she is waiting for your answer. ... Dear Papa is looking forward to receive a letter from you. What are you doing now, dear child? I hope you found work. After all you have your craft—and that should be of great value to you. Are you still with "the acquaintance?" Weather here is bad right now—rain and darkness, early night and black—you would not leave the house; yet one would like to see and hear more. We hope peace will come soon and that all mankind will be spared mischief. We hear often from our loved ones in "A" and are glad to hear good news. All mail to them goes faster now. I will close now, the letter has to be forwarded. We hope to hear from you soon "by this way" dear child. Be healthy—greetings to all loved ones, particularly to Aunt Jo and be you particularly kissed by your mother.

Thousands of greetings and kisses from your loving Vati.

Also for aunt Jo[12] [Side note]: For darling Hanni and Jo... (Signed) Hedwig.

A second letter reads:

My dear Hanni!

It is hard to express how much you comforted us with your letter—much time has passed. You are healthy and content, that is what counts. To this point we also are content; our dear Papi is merry and set at ease, now that he has read your notes, dear child. It appears that you meet Aunt Hanna daily; that is good. Otto is still at home. Sonja writes that she was confined to bed—appendicitis; but she feels better now. Otherwise, there is no specific news. Say hello to Aunt Hanna and all souls. But you, dear child, receive my kisses.

Mother!

Greetings and Kisses Papa!

Greetings from Tante Heddi (Hedwig)[13]

Lines added on postcard from Mommy and Papi, stamped on 5 April 1939 in Cologne, and addressed to:

Miss
Hanni Marx
8 Brokesley-Street
London E 3.
Bow.
England

Dear Hanni,

I have been waiting for a letter for a long time. How long are you going to let me wait? Hopefully I'll be hearing from you soon, thus, get better.[14] Regards and Kisses Luise.

After Jeannette left, life for her family in Germany became more and more impossible to endure. "By January 1940, rationing for Jews became more stringent, as they were denied legumes, most fruit, and meat. … The only recourse, for those with means, was the growing black market of foodstuffs."(6) Marianne comments in a letter to a relative [later forwarded to Jeannette]:

> Concerning telephones, there are some in neighborhood stores, but they are still closed, also the post office. In this house there are none. How about soap and coffee? Hopefully all things will soon be alright.

A letter from "Aunt Ilse" [15] seems to acknowledge she has received Marianne's request:

> One does not hear or see much. We will try to send coffee and soap to Köln. They ask for that. Right now the weather is beautiful, and we hope that our business will pick up; I can leave it only late evenings. ... I am just by myself and always in the evening when I have to do the commissions. It would be good to have you here; but over there it must be better still.

Lines added to letter by Aunt Hedwig:

> I'm down here[16] visiting with dear Mommy and Daddy. They are doing well, and I'm always very happy about your dear and funny letters. Make sure to always keep your humor, which you have inherited from your father. I'm doing so-so, and have become quite an old aunt. Other than that there is nothing of importance to report, and so I'm sending heartfelt regards to you today from Aunt Heddy.

The following letter was one of the last letters Jeannette received from her parents:.

1939/23

Tuesday, 20 February 40

My dear child,

We have received your dear letter, and as always were happy to read good things in it. You make no mention at all if you have received my letter, wherein we congratulated Aunt to her birthday, although somewhat belated. — Might our letters possibly have crossed yours? — The mail is taking longer due to the heavy snowfall, and so on, and regretfully one has to resign oneself to this situation. Hopefully it'll get warmer soon and improve, then this thing will be faster as well; and so don't assume that I'm too lazy to write — but if everything is delayed, tell me in your next letter if you have received the one dated 28 January. Why don't you once write together with Aunt Emilie, I think she would write much faster. What is Ilse doing, is she still employed? Give my regards to her. What is her husband doing? We are alright. The doctor is pleased with dear Dad so far. — [17] ... we are awaiting spring with longing. Aunt Heddi had an upset stomach again. Now she is better, but she has to watch how much she is eating. — I don't see Aunt Paula, etc., often, I don't have much time to visit. After all, you know how things are, dear child. Ine dropped by yesterday, she is going to preparatory training for her apprenticeship, Otto will be coming here as well. — I only see them here if something is to be had. — I never ever see Luise — oh well — why should she come here anyway. — You, dear child, know how they all are. Yesterday Mr. and Mrs. Moser left for Amsterdam — I gave them your address and you'll hear from them. Hopefully. Lore's dear father left for the USA last week. — Other than that there are hardly any news, my dear child, and chances are that you know all the news. I hear from Riga often, since it's extremely cold. Mr. Lehrefsky[18] is here right now and sends his regards to you, and his niece Rosemarie as well, whose acquaintance you have made via her mother, as we have heard from Mr. Leh. — How are things in regards to dances and the club? Hopefully you are quite enjoying yourself there. And so, please let me know if you have received all letters. My dear child, I'm hoping that you are in best of health when you receive these lines, just as I was when they left me. Please send my regards to dear Jo and Ilse, and to everyone. I'm sending most heartfelt kisses to you, and from your dear Daddy as well.

Your Mother who loves you from all her heart

Jeannette had some idea that life was worsening for her family still trapped in Germany, but she could not have fathomed the hell that was yet to come. Meanwhile, life pressed on in England when on February 16, 1940, London's *Evening Standard* displayed the headline:

HITLER'S GESTAPO EMPLOYING JEWS FOR SPYING IN ENGLAND!

Apparently, a Gestapo member confessed that the Nazis placed approximately 400 German spies in England. They bribed or blackmailed Jews seeking refuge in England to spy on the host country.(7) In May 1940, the British Government introduced a policy of mass internment of refugees. For several months, an intense newspaper campaign had been trying to mobilize public opinion against the German and Austrian refugees, branding all refugees as spies. Up until April, this campaign had apparently little effect; it was the fear and shock of the German military victories in May and June of 1940 that created a hostile atmosphere of panic and suspicion, leading to a flurry of Government anti-refugee measures. Jewish refugees were now viewed as "enemy aliens" and interned as such, with the prospect of being deported to Canada or Australia, along with enemy prisoners of war.(8)

The day arrived when Jeannette had to go in front of an English judge to obtain permission to stay in the country. "I was an enemy alien. I asked the policeman where the court was and he took me there. I was shaking. Then I had to wait there a long time." She had heard about other refugees being taken into custody so Jeannette was extremely nervous about what might happen to her.

"Jeannette Marx, please come with me, you're next." Jeannette was escorted into a room and seated in front of the judge who was quietly examining her documents. "He said to me, 'What's your name?' And I said, 'Jeannette Marx.' 'No, your name is Hanni Marx. What's your father's name?' 'Salomon Marx.' 'No, Sally Marx. What's your mother's name?'" By this time, Jeannette felt terribly worried and confused.

"How does he know so much about me and my family?" She hesitantly answered his question, "Marianne Marx." The judge looked her straight in the eye and said, "'No, Jenny Marx.'" Jeannette was dumbfounded. Afraid of what he might say next, her heart pounded. "He thinks I'm a spy! Then, he told me, 'Don't worry! You used to sit on my lap when you were little. I used to come to your house in the country and to your apartment in the city. Your mother and my wife became good friends. Your mother spoke perfect English,' he says … 'Your father spoke a little bit but not much so I had to speak German.'" The judge went on to describe the ranch and its exact location in Kleinvernich. Jeannette was astonished. "He says, 'I know who you are; you're okay. You can go to work now.'" Breathing a great sigh of relief, Jeannette watched as the judge scribbled something down on her ID card and handed it back to her. He had written: "Refugee from Nazi Oppression," and signed it: "*J.H. Thorpe*." The English judge she appeared in front of was none other than Colonel Thorpe of the British Army of Occupation. Jeannette recounts this unbelievable coincidence with a great laugh. While stationed in the Rhine, he had befriended Salomon after purchasing horses from him. "He was a colonel and purchased what they needed from my father for the army. Then he says to me, 'And we used to go to the opera together. Your mother and my wife enjoyed it and your father and I fell asleep.'"

After receiving permission to work, Jeannette gained employment in a military uniform factory. She kept herself busy by working hard and was fairing relatively well, until she received a letter from the United States. It was from her Cousin Kurt and the news was devastating:

Memphis, April 20th, 1941

Dear Hanni,

I have heard from my dear parents of the passing of your dear father, and am expressing my deepest sympathy to you. How sad that you were not able to see your dear father again one more time. His last years were filled with so much pain, so that we must not begrudge this rest to him, and have to thank God for it.

If it's God's will, you and your dear mother will soon be allowed to live together. Dear Hanni, hopefully you and all of our relatives are doing well.

Kindest regards and kisses from your cousin Kurt

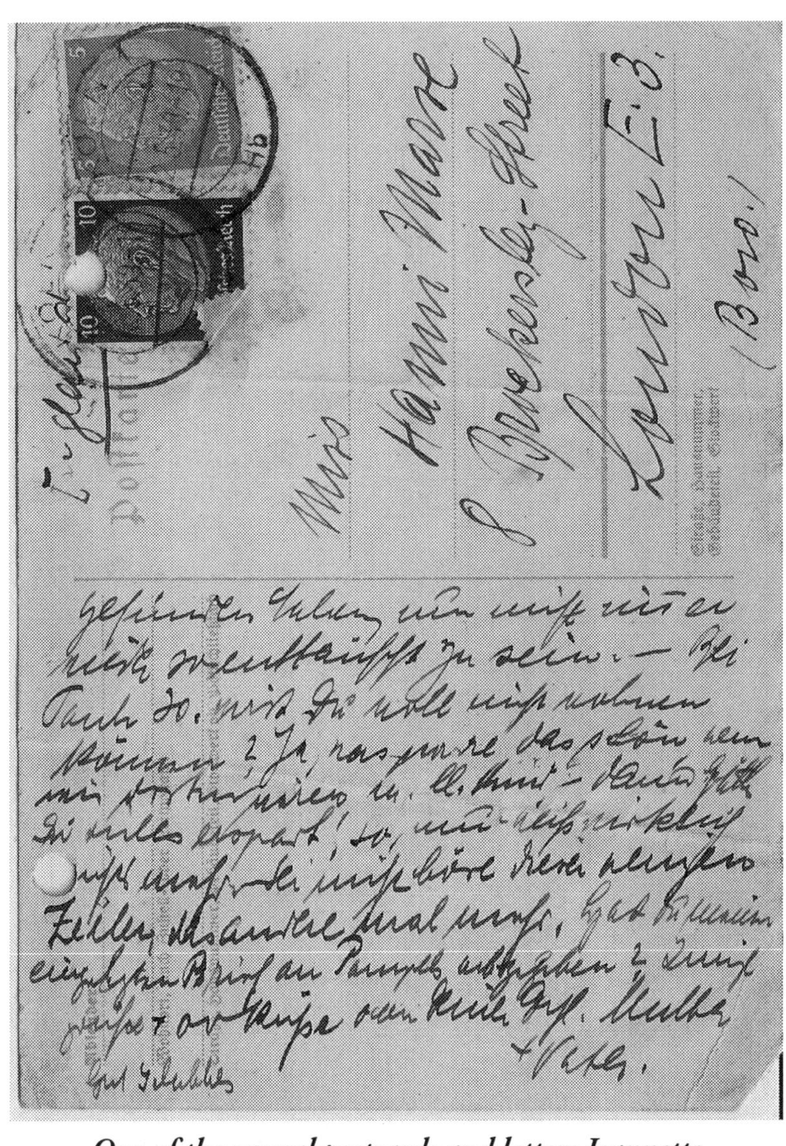

One of the several postcards and letters Jeannette received from her parents

Alien's Order, 1920—Certificate of Registration, issued by the Metropolitan Police Aliens Registration Office

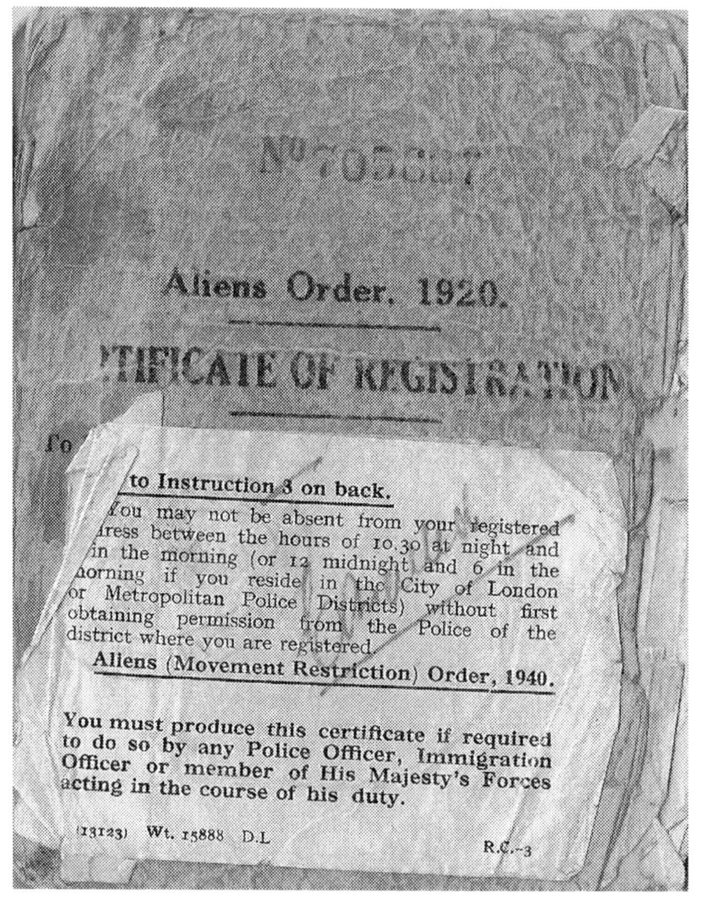

Aliens Order, 1920.

TIFICATE OF REGISTRATION

To

to Instruction 3 on back.

You may not be absent from your registered dress between the hours of 10.30 at night and in the morning (or 12 midnight and 6 in the morning if you reside in the City of London or Metropolitan Police Districts) without first obtaining permission from the Police of the district where you are registered.

Aliens (Movement Restriction) Order, 1940.

You must produce this certificate if required to do so by any Police Officer, Immigration Officer or member of His Majesty's Forces acting in the course of his duty.

(13123) Wt. 15888 D.L R.C.-3

NAME (Surname first in Roman Capitals)
MARX Jeannette

Nationality German
Born on 4/6/1921 in Cologne
Previous Nationality (if any)
Profession or Occupation
Single or Married Single
Address of Residence 384 Old Kent Rd
Arrival in United Kingdom on
Address of last Residence outside U.K.
Koln Germany
Government Service
Passport or other papers as to Nationality and Identity
H.O. Travel Document No. 214

Jeannette's Certificate of Registration

6

ENDORSEMENTS AND REMARKS.

Reported on 10/10/39.

METROPOLITAN POLICE
WEST HAMPSTEAD
10/10/39
"S" DIVISION

7

ENDORSEMENTS AND REMARKS

The holder of this Certificate is to be exempted until further order from internment and from the special restrictions applicable to enemy aliens under the Aliens Order, 1920, as amended, Refugee from Nazi oppression

METROPOLITAN POLICE
TRIBUNAL
No. 24
ALIENS REGISTRATION

J. H. Thorpe

29 NOV 1939

The Honorable J. H. Thorpe exempts Jeannette from internment and writes, "Refugee from Nazi Oppression"

15

"We'll Call You Frenchy"

Jeannette knew she would never again have the opportunity to see her father alive and she wept bitterly, even before receiving the news. Although Jeannette admits she is not exactly sure how her father died, Salomon apparently succumbed to health complications stemming from the injuries and paralysis he suffered from the assault. Before receiving the news, Jeannette remembers a profound sadness came over her out of the blue and she did not know why at the time. Once she received word her father died it made sense. Jeannette hurt intensely for her mother because she was missing not only her only child, but now her husband as well. How was she handling Salomon's death? How was she going to carry on without him? Where was she now? Jeannette had to suppress these haunting thoughts and keep fighting for her own survival. She needed to stay strong until it was all over and she could return home to be with Marianne.

"So I worked in a factory where they made military uniforms and I wanted to join up [with the military] and the guy says, 'You can't.' I says, 'Can I join part time?' So I joined the ambulance service. It was a voluntary service so what happened was I had to take some tests and I did very well. ... Someone told me I took the test better than some of the English girls. And then he said, 'Where would you want to go?' And I said, 'Where is it the worst?' 'In the East end on the docks.'"

> The bombs started falling around 4:00 p.m., Saturday, September 7, 1940. To the Rev'd Maurice Wood, watching aghast from near Big Ben, it was the "majestic orderliness" of the bomber fleet that

> impressed him most. Seconds later the East End disintegrated. ... By night the docks were blazing furiously and hundreds of the mean houses that surrounded them were in shattered ruins. ... The Surrey Commercial Dock was so fiercely ablaze that the Fire Officer signaled desperately; "Send all the bloody pumps you've got; the whole bloody world's on fire." Our brace warden, who for months had been swaggering about in his uniform, tin helmet cocked to one side, was cringing against the wall under the concrete steps, sobbing," wrote Mr. Kyle of Westham contemptuously. I never saw that man again.(1)

Most of those with defined jobs to do performed them bravely and to the best of their ability.

> The Germans returned to pound the same areas night after night. ... 171 bombers hit the East End on the night of Sept. 8th, killing 400. On 9 September 200 bombers came by day, 170 by night. Another 370 died. The following night saw the gutting of St. Katherine's Dock in what at that date some believed the worst fire England had ever known. All the warehouses surrounding the dock were destroyed in four or five hours.(2)

> Between 7 September and 13 November 1940, London was the main, almost the exclusive, target of the German raiders—27,500 high explosive bombs and innumerable incendiaries were dropped ... an average of 160 bombers attacked nightly: a figure reduced by bad weather—as on 2 November, the only raid-free night of the whole period—but greatly exceeded when the full moon and good weather coincided—as on 15 October when 410 raiders dropped 538 tons of high explosive bombs, killing 400 people.(3)

"So I was stationed in the slums near the docks where most of the bombs fell, where everything came first. I wanted to get against Hitler. That was one way to get back at him and I worked there until the war was finished. I was the only refugee there, more or less and it [the area] was rough."

On May 21, 1942, Jeannette reported for duty. Her station, 103, was located at 147 Cannon St. Road in the East End of London and she was assigned to ambulance 112. Jeannette worked for the London

Auxiliary Ambulance Service (L.A.A.S.) until July 1945, after the War ended. Jeannette was issued a uniform, which she promptly personalized. "The shoes didn't fit too good; they hurt. ... Nothing fit too well. We were in wartime, what are you gonna do? You do the best you can. See how fancy I made my shirt? I put my initials on it." She shows a photograph of herself with the initials "J" and "M" embroidered on her blouse. All personnel were issued protective gear that was kept in the ambulance. They were also issued "wet gear" to be used when fire fighters were putting out flames on scene. Large gas masks were mandatory and were different from those issued to the public. Black tin hats were for regular personnel while white hats were issued to senior officers.(3) Jeannette recalls proudly, "We wore the same hats the soldiers wore." Altogether 12 women were assigned to station 103 and they worked 48 hours on and 24 hours off. When there were no war-related emergency calls, L.A.A.S. personnel took routine accident or illness calls. First Aid courses were mandatory and personnel were taught that time was of the essence. One former L.A.A.S. volunteer describes it in this manner:

> We were instructed to rescue with all due speed and, after a quick assessment of the patient's injuries, prevent further damage. As the patients would be taken to the hospital immediately there was no need to dress superficial wounds or spend time applying elaborate bandages. Broken legs were stabilized in a rudimentary fashion by tying them together at the knees and ankles with arm slings. ... In the event of the intestines being exposed we were instructed to cover the abdomen with our tin hats "to keep infection out and the guts in."(4)

Ironically, Jeannette had never even driven a vehicle, yet she had to pass a detailed driving test before she could join the ambulance service. "I learned how to drive and there was a priest who used to teach us. He was the driving instructor. Not a Catholic one, a Protestant one ... a pastor. So we used to discuss religion, of course. It was interesting. He was very nice about it, especially when he found out where I came from. ... At night time he even took us out to make sure we knew how to drive in a blackout." As part of her driving test, "They put a pail of water in the back of the ambulance because the brakes weren't so good. They wanted to see how much you spilled. You see how primitive the ambulance was? We also had to learn how to fix engines. The ambulances were converted Fords and they put campers on them and they had four stretchers in there. You could hardly see. Everything was blacked out and there was just one slit in the front lights. The only light was when they had bombings. Well, you had to do the best you could. The window was open so you could see where you were going more or less but you had to go very slow."

In a book about her aunt's role in the London Auxiliary Ambulance Service, *The Forgotten Service*, Angela Raby describes:

> The ambulances, being conversions of commercial vans, were extremely uncomfortable with little springing. It was necessary to double declutch through the gears. During the Blitz, London was bombed every night until Christmas Eve when a lull lasted until New Year's Eve when incendiary bombs were dropped.(5)

To get a better understanding of what Jeannette and others like her experienced driving at night, *The Forgotten Service* explains, "The black-out was efficiently policed by the wardens who patrolled to make sure all sources of light were eliminated lest an enemy aircraft be guided by an errant beam. Traffic was only able to crawl because there was no street lighting and the use of normal headlights was forbidden. However the headlight had a louvered cover fitted which had an aperture the size of a shilling to allow a minute beam of light. Partially due to this fact, the speed limit for the ambulances was set at 16 m.p.h. Driving slowly over glass-strewn roads was mandatory lest a puncture occurred—a heinous crime."(6) Fortunately, Jeannette never punctured a tire or had any accidents and her excellent driving skills earned her Certificate of Merit awards.

Ambulance Station 103 was a converted gas station. Because gas lines were below it, the ambulance personnel could not use it as a shelter during air raids. "The ambulance station—you couldn't even stay in that. It was built above a garage so we had to sleep behind the ambulances in the back. We all slept in one area. When there was no raid on we could sleep above the ground shelter, otherwise we slept behind the trucks and then we drew lots. One person could sleep in the ambulance that was never used ... only if there would be any gas bombs or something. We slept on stretchers anyway. We didn't have beds or anything it was primitive, very primitive."

"There was a house on the premises and the station officer's office was located here. When a call-out was received on the phone, personnel would run to retrieve their orders from this office. We had to go up to the office and they gave us the orders. We were in the worst neighborhood and there were food lines. We had to see that they didn't block our station. The house also contained a bathroom and a kitchen but not laundry services." On Jeannette's day off she took the subway back to the hostel and washed her clothes there. "We could take a bath or a shower every day if we wanted to. We had a dining area, you know, we ate there. We had a cook, a Cockney, and she always made me such good cups of coffee. She boiled the milk and mixed it with the coffee grounds. I wanted to have tea with the Aussies because their tea was really black. We had a dairy close by so we could have fresh milk but eggs and meat were rationed so we got spam and all that stuff from the States. I didn't like it but I ate it. … If you're hungry you'll eat anything," During the day if there were no call-outs, "we had to clean the cars then clean where we stayed. We were always busy doing things. On a typical day we wouldn't wake up because we were busy all night. We wouldn't even get to sleep."

One had to obtain written permission to take a leave of absence. The only time Jeannette took leave was when she had her tonsils removed. After that, she was struck with appendicitis and subsequently had her appendix removed. Regarding her hospital stay Jeannette recalled, "I got better food than the rest because if you were in the service you got different food."

With great disdain, Jeannette describes what Station 103's first officer in charge was like: "The funny thing is I never forget because with white gloves she checked inside the motor to see if everything was clean!" When she wasn't performing "white glove" inspections on ambulance engines, she would send Jeannette and co-worker Lena out at night to perform map exercises. Lady Deller refused to allow them to complete the map exercises in the ambulances because they "had to save gas." Instead, she insisted the young women walk alone in the pitch dark to find locations she selected beforehand. "She said you had to go there and there and there and there, you know … stupid.

You don't send two young girls out. So we went into a fish and chips restaurant. We asked the guy where's this, this, this [gesturing as if she were pointing to a map]. Surprised, the man asked, 'They make you two walk around? Sit down, I'll tell you exactly where it is; you're not walkin' around!' He sat down with us and was very nice … he even gave us a cup of tea."

Lena and Jeannette became best friends and served together until the War was over. In regard to Lady Deller, a perfect opportunity presented itself for Jeannette to experience a little "poetic justice" of her own. "One day [Lady Deller] had company and we had to bring tea and I forgot the spoon so I … you know [uses her index finger to show how she stirred the fine Lady's tea]." Jeannette cheekily defended herself: "She used to go with white gloves over the motors! Remember I told you, she was crazy." Besides, Jeannette points out, "She became a Lady because her husband, who was a businessman, was made a Lord. She wasn't born that way … like we had girls in my outfit who were born that way."

In time, Lady Deller left Station 103 and was replaced by Dorothy Freyer, a school teacher whom Jeannette highly respected. The second officer-in-charge turned out to be the manager of well-known concert pianist, Joan Davies. Ms. Davies, who volunteered her time as an L.A.A.S volunteer at Station 39, used to drop in to visit her.(7) Jeannette recalls, "When Joan Davies came to the station, she had two poodles and I used to take them for a walk."

With Ms. Freyer now in charge, station 103 was a bit more relaxed when the bombs weren't falling. Off duty, Jeannette volunteered her time mentoring the East End's poor children, some of whom became orphans when their parents were killed during the raids. "On down time, I went next door to the club for the children and tutored them. Well, I had an accent so the children wanted to know where I was from." Jeannette did not like explaining to the children or even to other personnel that she was a Jewish refugee from Germany. Her Australian friend and fellow ambulance driver Gwen Ridley offered this advice: 'You know, Jeannette, you have a French name, you speak French, tell them you're French, we'll call you Frenchy.' So from then on, Jeannette became known to friends and strangers alike as Frenchy, a nickname that suited her spunky personality quite well.

London, 1942 Photograph of Station 103. L.A.A.S. members from left to right are Luisa, Gwen Ridley, Eileen Rowlinson, Eileen Sanders, Jeannette, and Elsie Green.

14

ENDORSEMENTS AND REMARKS

Business Address.

METROPOLITAN POLICE HAMPSTEAD 20.9.41 "S" DIVISION

PERMISSION GRANTED FOR EMPLOYMENT AS Ambulance Driver

WITH Station 149

SUBJECT TO REVIEW AS NECESSARY

2 APR 1942

GERMAN AND AUSTRIAN EMPLOYMENT EXCHANGE,
HANOVER HOUSE,
73/76, HIGH HOLBORN, W.C.1.

15

ENDORSEMENTS AND REMARKS

METROPOLITAN POLICE HAMPSTEAD "S" DIVISION

Business Address
Ambulance Stn. 103
Stepney E.
18.6.42

METROPOLITAN POLICE HAMPSTEAD 19.6.42 "S" DIVISION

No Occupation
4/7/48 from 2/4/45

METROPOLITAN POLICE HAMPSTEAD "S" DIVISION

Jeannette received written permission to officially join the London Auxiliary Ambulance Service

L.A.A.S. member and artist "SAX"'s rendition of "learning to drive."

Jeannette in the L.A.A.S., 1943

16

"We Were Scared to Death"

The Nazis assaulted London with a variety of air artillery. They used high explosive bombs as well as oil-filled bombs that caught fire as soon as they hit the ground. Another sinister weapon was "the land mine which floated down on a parachute until a solid object was reached." London referred to these as "Molotov Bread Baskets."[(1)] By 1944, the Germans developed unmanned missiles, or V1's. These bombs were in the shape of an airplane and designed so that when the engine stopped, the bomb glided down, which gave only a slight warning to those on the ground. The Nazis launched between 100 and 150 each day.[(2)] One former B.B.C. employee described it this way: "The V1's were, I thought, far more nerve-wracking. With the V2's you either were or were not on the receiving end. If they went off and you were alive, you were all right. But with the V1's you never knew where they would drop and the suspense from the time you heard their engines chugging over to the actual explosion was a real war of nerves."[(3)] Jeannette remembers, "All of a sudden, BOOM! Like the Easter holidays and the Jewish holidays were together and soldiers were on leave, some of them, and they got all ... bombed ... with the V2's. They were so fast you know like, *Whew!* [making a quick whistling sound] then *Boom!* The other ones were like little airplanes, the doodlebugs. You saw like little airplanes, we would see where they were going to go—our way or the other way. You have no choice, sometimes you see them and sometimes it happens. Terrible! You don't know where they're gonna fall ... they could fall on top of you ... they could fall anywhere. If you're standing somewhere—you don't know. They were so fast anyway … you lived on time, either you get killed or not get killed, that's all. It's up to God."

When Jeannette and other personnel received a call-out, "There was no time to panic. Listen, it wasn't easy but we did what we had to do. We were scared to death but we did it. Nobody else was doing it." Jeannette describes, in a matter-of-fact tone, and without much detail, the first call she ever had. It "was a regular bombing and I saw a lot of blood for the first time. I put on tourniquets and everything and I did what I had to do. I was expecting it. When they taught you first aid they told you this is what's going to happen. If they're dead, they're dead; you have to take them to the mortuary, which I didn't like. I wasn't the only one, I think."

Angela Raby describes:

> It is difficult fifty years on to comprehend fully the gruesome content of their work, given the current experiences of a modern ambulance service. Not only responding to emergencies through air raids but collecting casualties with appalling injuries was doubly awful when these were civilians. A description of the collection of dismembered bodies, often rat-eaten, elicited a casual remark that people would not believe how heavy a severed leg was to lift. … Transporting these assorted bits and pieces of bodies to the largest refrigeration system in London, turned one ambulance driver against fish for years. Nevertheless, humour was the catalyst that kept these crews cemented together, and obliterated, at least for awhile, the horror.(4)

As a first aid medic and ambulance driver, there was one location Jeannette tried to avoid as much as possible: the mortuary. She did not like taking bodies there, so she quickly gained a reputation at the local hospital for transporting patients who were beyond medical help. "When the bombs were falling we had to come pick up the people and take them to the hospital or the mortuary, and I didn't like to go to the mortuary, so they used to tell me, 'Frenchy, are they dead or are you making them alive?'" Jeannette would respond, "'They were still alive when I saw them last. You'll have to ask my attendant.' Because I didn't like to drop them off there, [the hospital staff] knew me already." Every time Jeannette made a trip to the hospital, the staff first made sure Jeannette's patients were alive before lifting them out of the ambulance.

Remembering the psychological difficulty Jeannette explains, "It was terrible! All those people with their wounds and everything. We had to do first aid and take them to the hospital. … I hated the mortuary because of dead people. We had to carry them in on a stretcher. Bodies, sometimes pieces. Kids, children everything. Some died on us … we were so busy we had to come back right away to pick up more people. It gave us no chance to talk to them, the few seconds we had it was just, 'You'll go to the hospital and they're gonna do everything for you, we're doing the best we can now, you know.' We had no time. You wanted to get them there as fast as possible." Jeannette adds with a bit of humor, "If they weren't dead they thanked us for helping them."

Jeannette experienced an unforgettably terrifying event one evening while on duty, although she recounts the experience without much emotion or detail. "It was pitch dark and we were on our way to a call and we had to keep a good distance. I was driving and they were bombed. The ambulance in front of us was blown up … it was terrible. I was hit by a German fragment. It went through the roof, on my helmet and out the window. I went to the hospital because I got hit but in those days if you get a shock on the head it wasn't anything. Nowadays they find out it was really something. I wasn't bleeding so I went back to work. I had a headache for a month!" When pressed for more information Jeannette aptly responds, "I blocked it out completely. I don't like to live on the bad things; I like to live on the good things." The ambulance she was following was driven by girls from her own station; two co-workers she, of course, knew very well. Both ambulances were under attack by the Nazis but they missed Jeannette's. The ambulance ahead of her suddenly blew up, instantly killing her friends right before her eyes. Jeannette brings out and shows a heavy, palm-sized shard of German shrapnel. "This came through the ambulance window. I got other pieces from the side of my ambulance." Active duty does not allow a person much time for reflection or to grieve the loss of dear friends; as soon as she was released from the hospital, Jeannette was right back to work.

Driving at night in a blackout was extremely challenging, but when fog was added to the equation, one had to rely on her other senses. "During the day if the roads were alright you drove faster; at night time you didn't know how the roads were. It's easy to get lost in a blackout, especially when it was foggy. What happened was, it was a foggy night and we had casualties. [Jeannette was backing the ambulance out.] Some Americans, they were stationed also on the port you know, so one of them says, 'Go back.' I says, 'I can't go back.' 'Go back!' he said again. I says, 'I can't go back!' And you know what? I was that much over [uses both hands to show about a foot in length]. A little more I would've been in the water. He didn't realize it. I figured (to myself), that's not good, I don't think that that's right, let me stop it. I had a feeling, sometimes you get a feeling. I says, I'm not gonna go back, I'm gonna look first. I had to take the flashlight [to see in the fog] and I was that much over, you know off the edge. I was used to picking up people on the docks so I knew more than he did. He apologized to me. 'You're right,' he said. I said, 'I know the neighborhood you don't know it yet. When you're here longer you'll realize it.' I almost fell off the dock and the ambulance had four people in there!"

"Another time I was talking to somebody and I says, 'Get down! Get down!' You know it was also on the docks and we were waiting to get the casualties to pick up and he got hit because he didn't go down. I went under the ambulance and he stayed up. The Americans took him away so I don't know what happened to him. I heard something and I got down as fast as I could."

Another close call came when Jeannette and her attendant were called out to transport a heavy patient. "Then when we'd get heavy people we'd call someone else to help. There was one person that was so heavy that four of us had to go in one ambulance. We had to drop the patient off at the hospital, then back out. We kept trying but couldn't get the ambulance to back up. I don't know, maybe more than a hundred yards, stupid, no? But I was lucky because that saved us … we just didn't make it. Because the bridge blew up. We heard the doodlebugs, we didn't know what it was and all of a sudden we hear, *BOOM!* And thank God it didn't happen to us. If we would've been faster it would've been us." The Nazis dropped a doodlebug destroying the bridge Jeannette would have been crossing had she not had to back out of the hospital, which, of course, took longer. As stated previously, humor, especially dry, oftentimes even dark, was often used to ease tension during the war. Sometimes, civilians themselves found humor in tragedy as former L.A.A.S. member Joan Windsor recounts:

> There were some real characters around in the Civil Defense—East Enders who were taxi drivers or market traders, unable to go to war because they were too old, etc. They were fun. I was at Cannonbury Road one night and it had been particularly busy. We all reported back and one man, a real character, a trader in Petticoat Lane, came back laughing. We asked him what was so funny and he relayed how a house had fallen down and they'd dug a bloke out. Apparently, once rescued he said, "I thought it was a bit strange, I was only sitting on the toilet, I pulled the chain and the house fell down!"That is a story that has stuck in my mind. We did laugh about that.[(5)]

Humor also played a strange role for those Jews still trapped in Germany, as captured in one of Victor Klemperer's journal entries in *I Will Bear Witness.* He writes, "We make jokes and laugh and are basically all in despair."[(6)]

The most heart-wrenching incident Jeannette responded to was located in Bethnal Green, an area in the East End of London. Civilians living there were startled by rocket sounds nearby so dozens of them scrambled to take cover. "There was a bomb shelter. There was a bomb nearby but they ran into the shelter and fell on top of each other. That was the worst. They suffocated. That was the worse thing. When you see bombs do it and it happens that way it's terrible but when they run and they get killed … We had to go in and take them out. The wounded on top we took to the hospital and the others we had to take to the mortuary. We had to go down and one fell on top of the other because they panicked. It wasn't a false alarm but they weren't hit … and we had so many casualties without them being hit directly. People were trying to enter the shelter and it was so deep … they killed themselves. That was near my station, the East End was very, very … you know, poor neighborhoods are always crowded, a lot of people lived there. We felt terrible, especially because there was no bombs or anything, you know. We were there as the first station on the scene. We had to take in the ambulance, you know, back and forth and women from other stations came there too … because there were too many people there, can you imagine? That was something you can't ever forget. They panicked, just panicked."

In *London at War*, Philip Ziegler describes this tragedy:

> The most macabre incident of 1943 was, however, only indirectly due to enemy action. It happened in Bethnal Green, on the night of 3 March, during a minor raid in which no bombs fell in the neighbourhood. People were filing decorously into the tube station when a salvo of rockets was fired from nearby Victoria Park. The official enquiry established that there had been no real panic but people outside undoubtedly pressed forward so as to get under cover. A woman near the top of the steep staircase, with a child or bundle in her arms, slipped and fell on to the people in front of her, who in turn lost their balance. The staircase was 'converted from a corridor into a charnel house in from ten to fifteen seconds,' said Laurence Dunne, the magistrate who conducted an enquiry into the affair; 178 people were crushed to death or suffocated. 'The disaster was caused by a number of people losing their self-control at a particularly unfortunate place and time,' said Dunne. No individual was to blame, no one had behaved notably badly, not much could be done to stop it happening again except by the use of common-sense and restraint.[7]

Jeannette's experiences with the L.A.A.S. are marked with fond memories as well as very sorrowful ones. First Officer Dorothy Freyer's leadership was one such fond memory.

"She was terrific and we had to transfer two German soldiers (POW's), you know, and she says to me, 'Jeannette, I'm not gonna send you. You do the office work, I'll send the others. I don't know what you're gonna do to them.' She didn't want to hurt *me*. I thought that was very, very nice." First Officer Freyer treated Jeannette and the other girls very well and after the War ended and Jeannette was leaving, she gave her a gold bracelet and some money to help her begin a new life. Another fond moment came when Jeannette was delivering payroll to the stations in the area. "What happened was I drove. Two men went also and we paid all the stations.

"So I go to an all mans station and they say, 'You know, Frenchy, have you ever had Irish coffee?' I says, 'No.' … I started to laugh and laugh. Something was wrong with me and I was a little bit dizzy … so they had to get someone else to drive. They were reprimanded."

Jeannette also recounts that she and other girls from her station were invited to perform a dance routine in an armed services show "with costumes and everything." The show was a welcome break from the hardships of serving during wartime. Meeting royalty, however, was quite the icing on the cake … yet Jeannette was not overly impressed. "We were recommended [for a commendation] for all of the things we did. We were [serving in] one of the worst areas and the King and Queen came to visit us, you know. At the station, we stood at, what do you call it? attention and that's how you meet them. They're very cold, the British." Apparently the pomp and circumstance didn't sit very well with Jeannette.

In May 1942, "The Greatest Air Raid in History," according to the British Press, took place. More than 1,000 bombers released 15 tons of explosives over Jeannette's hometown, Cologne. The heart of the city was completely destroyed but the Cologne Cathedral, although hit several times, remained towering high and intact.[(8)] This devastating news greatly disturbed Jeannette as she had no idea whether or not her mother or the rest of her family still lived in Cologne. What's worse, she had not received word from them in a long time and had absolutely no way of getting in touch with them. Still, she continued dutifully serving in the L.A.A.S until the war was over and Germany surrendered. In regard to her brave service during the War Jeannette observes, "I was the driver and the medic and I had an attendant. If my life didn't change in Germany, I would have been a doctor."

The *New York Times* headline on Wednesday, May 2, 1945 announced:

HITLER DEAD IN CHANCELLERY, NAZIS SAY; DOENITZ, SUCCESSOR, ORDERS WAR TO GO ON

"LONDON, May 1—Adolf Hitler died this afternoon, the Hamburg radio announced tonight, and Grand Admiral Karl Doenitz, proclaiming himself the new Fuehrer by Hitler's appointment, said that the war would continue."[9] "News tickers in the House of Commons lobby carried the news of Hitler's death … But there was an almost complete lack of excitement here. Those who believed the report seemed to accept it as a matter of course that Hitler would die. There was no official reaction."[10] Jeannette was elated that the war was finally over. It would soon be confirmed that the vile dog of a man who robbed her of childhood dreams and tore her family to pieces, now lay dead.

A few days later, on May 7, 1945, the BBC announced: "Germany has signed an unconditional surrender bringing to an end six years of war in Europe, according to reports from France."[11]

"The CO [commanding officer] told us over the intercom, 'The war is over!' The war was finished and the pub next door came over to invite us in, they all knew us." "'I'll have some cider,'" Jeannette told the bartender. "'That's fine,'" he said with a grin.

"I never knew cider had alcohol in it. That was the second time I got drunk," Jeannette recalls with a smile.

After all that she had endured, Jeannette proved herself to be a resilient young woman.

During the war, Jeannette served bravely and maintained the mental fortitude to carry out her duties until the Nazi regime was finally crushed. She also carried psychological trauma that, unknown to her, surfaced every so often. Years later, a friend asked Jeannette if she was aware that every time a plane flew overhead, she flinched. Sadly, her best friend, Lena, who served alongside Jeannette during the war, would not fair so well. Jeannette explains: "An English girl named Lena became my best friend. She had the most beautiful red hair and she was very sweet." Soon after the war, Lena became depressed and could not break free from it. Distraught and hopeless, young Lena took her own life. "It was too hard for her, you know, they never talked about it then but it was post-traumatic stress." L.A.A.S. members received a service ribbon along with a beautifully written letter of recognition from the London County Council, which stated in part:

> That the Council places on record its high appreciation of the devotion to duty of all its staff, whether past or present, full-time or part-time, permanent or temporary, paid or unpaid, who,

> during the six years of the Second World War, 1939-1945, have performed such splendid work, often at great personal sacrifice and risk, both in the civil defence and kindred services administered by the Council and also in the Council's own normal services which have had to be maintained despite all circumstances of war.[(12)]

The Defense Medal was to soon follow, but Jeannette never received hers.

L.A.A.S. member and artist "SAX" humorously captures the quandary of transporting heavy patients

Jeannette next to her best friend, Lena (wearing the bandana). Above her is Elsie Green.

Cologne, Germany — Cpl. Luther E. Boger, Concord, N.C., sky trooper, reads a warning sign in the street. This street leads to the Rhine River and is under observation of the Germans who occupy a stronghold there. Cpl. Boger is with the 82nd Airborne Division.

4 April 1945. The German tank is burnt out and the torsion bars have been destroyed by the immense heat of the fire.

17

Bitter Tears and Rays of Hope

After the war ended and her ambulance service was over, Jeannette needed to find employment once again. She of course wanted to return to Germany and be reunited with her family. That is, until she received an unexpected and shocking letter from her first boyfriend, Rudi Billig. Rudi, a concentration camp prisoner, recounted his traumatic experiences at the hands of the Nazis. He then informed Jeannette that her mother, Marianne, along with her other relatives, did not survive the Holocaust. Rudi explained that he personally saw Marianne in Theresienstadt.[19] As Jeannette relives getting this sorrowful news from Rudi, she states, "And you know something, it's funny … when I was … one day I started to cry so bitterly over nothing. I'm not a crier, you know, I'm not a cry baby and … I didn't know why and then I realized, my father … another time I cried it must've been my mother. I felt it." Rudi would later write a follow-up letter, unsure if Jeannette received his first letter. In this second letter, he would give a first-hand account of the horrors and the profound loss he faced in the death camps.

Simmern, March 12th, 1946

Dear Hanni,

I don't know if you have received my first letter sent through HIAS in Frankfurt, that's why I'm writing this second letter to you. Sorry to say, I didn't meet our "letter carrier" Hans Forst last week, and subsequently I haven't heard from my relatives in quite a while, and I'll have to forward this letter through someone else as well. — You can imagine how happy I was about your letter! I imagined myself suddenly back in time when in training before my apprenticeship, and then remembered the times we spent together, which despite the problems were nothing compared to what followed. The time before the evacuation was filled with worries,[20] trying to find passage on a ship, and such. I have a vague recollection that you left for England back then. Until the day of my deportation I worked as a welder and had gotten quite good at it. I worked in Kalt, where Rolf Herzberg lived back then. I would like to give you a short account of the last years, until my liberation. My parents and my brother Oskar and I, were sent to Riga in the 3rd transport. Your cousin Ine, as well as Otto Seligmann and his mother, were among us as well. [Otto died at the Riga Ghetto from a disease, his mother later on at the military hospital, and Ine was present in one of the usual actions at the end of 1943]. While I was immediately transported to a work camp not far from Riga together with many young people, most everyone else remained at the Ghetto. In this first "work camp," where we were brought solely for extermination, I got to know hunger for the first time, and in all variations. I was very lucky in succeeding to be sent to Riga with a group of craftsmen, and then finally to my family, once about 1200 of 1800 in the work camp had perished [after about 6 months]. We remained at the Ghetto until the end of 1943, and we persevered despite the hunger. Sadly, we were then sent to different concentration camps in the Riga area, and men and women were separated. In these inhuman conditions most everyone perished. Hunger, cold, and mistreatment, were the order of the day. But despite all of this I would have succeeded in helping my parents, if only the terrible murders wouldn't have taken place in summer of 44. Everyone over 50 years of age was ordered to appear, and a little bit later everyone older than 30. Among them were my dear parents, and many acquaintances.

Thereafter Oskar and I were sent by ship to Stutthoff, close to Danzig, and later to Buchenwald, and then to Zeitz in Thuringia. Shortly before the Americans arrived we were transported eastwards again, the destination unknown. Escape[21] was unthinkable, besides that we didn't know if the news were authentic. Sadly my brother lost his life in a bombing raid, while I, together with a few others, was liberated in Theresienstadt on May 6 by the Red Army, following a 2 week odyssey through

> Czechoslovakia. After I had also successfully survived spotted fever we remained in Theresienstadt for a while, where we recovered rather quickly. In short, I returned to Cologne and met up there with a friend, Heinz Bärmann from Simmern, and so the two of us traveled to Simmern at the Hunsrück. Meanwhile Heinz has gotten married [Margrit Kohlmann from Cologne, formerly Wesel]. I live together with both of them in their parental house, which was the best solution for us. We are operating a car transport business since December, a job we are quite good at. We want to keep it up until our emigration. I'm in contact with my sister in Palestine, and also with my relatives in America – my cousins Helmut and Otto Marx, formerly at Marsilstein 5, are going to provide my affidavit. By the way, my Uncle Bernhard in Redford was the first with whom I was able to make contact again. Sadly I cannot share any pleasant news with everyone, and with you neither, dear Hanni. I would have preferred that 1000 times.
>
> Well, enough of all of this, and I don't even know if you are alright with everything I wrote. I also don't want to bring up the past any more, since what happened can't ever be fixed again. Let's hope that a better fate awaits us after these Zores. – Now to you, dear Hanni, please write sometimes.[22(1)]

Along with the rest of the world, Jeannette would only begin to comprehend the heinous atrocities committed by Hitler and the Nazis as the liberating soldiers reported back the horrors they encountered at the camps they were liberating. Many of these men, even though hardened by the ravages of war, became physically ill at the overwhelming evidence of large-scale torture and genocide. Not many survivors were found in these camps and, of those who were liberated, besides Rudi, no other friends or relatives of Jeannette who had stayed behind in Germany survived. For her, the truth that her precious mother was among the six million Jews that were murdered was so unspeakably devastating, she ceased to believe in God's existence. But as dreadful as it was to continue her young life without her mother and other family members, she had to pick up the pieces and continue on. After all, she was a *survivor.*

"You try to wipe the bad things out of your mind, but what can you do? It's unbelievable what people can do to other people."

Jeannette still needed to support herself and had to come up with a plan for her future, as bleak as it seemed at the time. "I did not want to go back to dressmaking so I went to take a typing test [to go to school] but I just couldn't type, I couldn't do it. ... I couldn't [concentrate] you know, it must have been post-traumatic too. Another girl with me, she was also in the service, she couldn't do the same. We were the only ones who couldn't really concentrate and do things, you know... the heck with it. Then my Aunt Hanna, who was a housekeeper, had a restaurant and she helped out and got paid. She always had her own restaurant in Germany already and she opened one up with friends in England and I used to work there. Even Eisenhower ate there! It was right near the American Consulate and everything. She had very good international food, continental. Aunt Hanna listened to my uncle; she sold her business in Germany and got out. Then I wanted to get a job to work with the kids and everything. They asked me, 'Are you British, are you educated?' 'No,' I said. You know what, forget about it. It was good enough for me to work 24 hours and 48 hours and pick up the pieces of people but now you're asking me what's what." Jeannette describes her frustration trying to gain employment in post-war England. "I wrote to my cousin [Werner] and he sent me an affidavit to work in the States." After working at the restaurant with Aunt Hanna, Jeannette decided to come to the States because, as she puts it, "I couldn't get a decent job and I didn't want to go back to dressmaking."

There was an irony to this, however. "So I decided to come to the U.S. and I went into dressmaking again," Jeannette explains with amusement, adding, "Well, I had no choice." Before her departure, Aunt Hanna threw her a going-away party and Uncle Benno was one of the guests in attendance.

At the party, Uncle Benno was there but Gudrun was out of town, "so he sat down and talked to me. The first time we really sat down, and he says, 'I didn't know you were that smart.' I says, 'You know, apples don't fall far from the tree.' He must have done well working for the English government because he had a beautiful home and everything and he got his money out too, probably, you know. Then after the war was over and I came to the States, I found out he worked with the English and American government under the Marshall Plan to rebuild Germany."

Indeed, Benedikt Marx played an extremely vital role regarding the fate of Germany as documented by Klaus H. Schulte:

> Already before the final destruction and conquest of the Third Reich, the victors had given thought to the occupation and their political involvement to come. A Jew took part, directly and indirectly, in these discussions that were so important to Germany. In 1944 the American Secretary of Treasury Henry Morgenthau Jr. had submitted a plan to President Roosevelt, planning to carve up Germany. Industrial complexes were to be removed in their entirety, and the divided German states turned into farmland. ... Michael Marx from Vernich had a son, Benedikt Marx, who had been appointed to the Board of Directors of the Worker's Bank in Berlin in 1919. Thereafter he was voted into the Council of Economic Advisors of the Empire. Until 1933 he was the Executive Officer of the Nationwide Association of Bank Employees. He then emigrated to England, and became Advisor to Foreign Minister Bevin, and in that capacity was able to influence plans for the defeated Germany. He was indeed involved in swaying the British Foreign Minister, and Sir Winston, to reject the Morgenthau Plan, which would have been very disadvantageous for Germany. This Vernich Economic Expert died in 1956 in Bad Godesberg.(2)

Jeannette could not fathom why her uncle wanted to participate in the restoration of Germany. She did know that she no longer wanted anything to do with the country of her birth. "My cousins sent me an affidavit, both of them; the one in New York [Werner] and the one in Alabama [Kurt]." In Werner's very patriotic and eloquently written Affidavit of Support he states the following:

> Honorable Sir:
>
> Enclosed you will please find Affidavit of Support, together with various papers required for the immigration of my cousin, Miss Jeannette Marx to the United States.
>
> Miss Marx and I grew up together in Cologne, Germany, and when we first became old enough to become aware of and to understand the meaning of fascism, we wanted to leave Germany and come to the United States. I was fortunate enough to come to this country nine years

> ago and have since done everything possible to be a loyal, faithful, and conscientious American, and to deserve the privilege of being a citizen of this great nation.
>
> Jeannette Marx left Germany in 1938 and has been in London for over seven years. During the war years, it was, of course, impossible for her to come to this country. Nevertheless, she has done her share and has contributed heavily toward the Victory that was ultimately to be ours. She was an Ambulance Driver and Social Welfare Worker in London's East End on a 24 hour duty call. She was constantly exposed to danger and often helped many when they were not able to help themselves.
>
> I feel that I have a moral duty to bring Miss Marx to this country and I am willing to assume full responsibility that at no time will she become a public charge to any community in the United States. I am certain that a girl of the caliber of Jeannette Marx will make the type of American citizen that this country can be proud of. I would very much appreciate it if you could issue an Immigration Visa to Miss Marx at your earliest convenience, as I am convinced that she will make a good and loyal American. Her quota number is 156.

On the ship, Jeannette shared a cabin with her friend Ruth Hertz who lived in the same hostel as she in England. Although their ship arrived in Ellis Island on Sunday, they had to wait until Monday to disembark. While on the ship Jeannette gazed out at the Statue of Liberty. Her life was about to begin again in a brand-new country; would it be a good one? Werner, Jeannette's sponsor, was so determined to put the past behind him, he changed his first and last names completely and now went by *Alfred Shaw*. When Jeannette arrived at Ellis Island, she was pleasantly surprised that Alfred was accompanied by a friend of hers she knew from the hostel. This friend, "who arrived in New York before me, got me a place in Washington Heights in New York where there were German Jews."

Arriving on Monday, Jeannette wasted no time applying for her Social Security card. By Wednesday, she was working as a dressmaker. "I got a job with a designer and made a living that way. My lunch was an apple, and dinner I ate because I had relatives in town.

The year was 1947 and Jeannette was 26 when the roommate she lived with in New York introduced her to a painter, a nice Jewish boy named Theodore Grunfeld. Like Jeannette, Theodore, too, had had to leave the country of his birth because of Hitler. Although born in New York, Theodore's father, David, was just six weeks old when his parents decided to return to Hungary. Once Hitler came to power, Theodore's father took his family and returned to New York. Theodore and Jeannette went out on a few dates, fell in love, and were married six weeks later. Her cousin Alfred gave her away in what must have been a bittersweet ceremony without her parents by her side.

Jeannette was disappointed that her father-in-law had not chosen Rabbi Kober to perform her marriage ceremony. After all, she knew Rabbi Kober from her childhood days in Cologne. Rabbi Kober had also escaped to England as Jeannette discovered when she bumped into him there: Ironically, shortly after arriving in New York, Jeannette was sitting on the steps of a library when, to her great surprise, she spotted Rabbi Kober walking down the street towards her. It was a moving second reunion.

After they married, the couple stayed with Theodore's parents until they could afford an apartment of their own. Theodore had his own business as a painter. After living in the apartment, they saved enough money to get a house in the Bronx.

Jeannette's co-worker from the L.A.A.S contacted her in the U.S. to let her know Joan Davies was going to perform in New York, and that she was invited to attend.

"Me and my husband sat right next to Mrs. Roosevelt! You know, my friend Joan, she said, 'Do me a favor, I won't be able to send flowers to Mrs. Roosevelt, and she gave me her address and everything.' I ordered a beautiful bouquet of flowers. My friend told her that she asked me to send the flowers and she said, 'They're beautiful.' I've met famous people you know," Jeannette says with a laugh.

On October 2, 1950, Jeannette gave birth to a baby boy, Stephen Michael, nicknamed "Steve," who would grow up to become a physician—the dream his mother once held for herself.

On October 15, 1951, the Grunfeld family welcomed a beautiful baby girl to the family and named her Marilyn. Jeannette recalls reading bedtime stories to her children and Steve started to call his baby sister

Bunny because it was easier to pronounce. To this day, Jeannette speaks to Bunny every day by phone and visits her regularly. Although German is her native language, Jeannette did not want to teach her children how to speak it. "I had such a bad feeling about Germany" on account of "what they did to my whole family."

Jeannette had no intention of returning to Germany, but Tante Hanna did. While there, she commissioned a headstone to honor both Salomon and Marianne. Later, Jeannette sent for Tante Hanna to live with her in New York.

More than forty years after the Holocaust, Jeannette received an invitation from the mayor of Cologne to return to her birthplace. In 1993, the city of Cologne invited her, along with other Holocaust survivors, to attend a ceremony in their honor. After giving it much thought, Jeannette decided to face the past and return. A good friend of hers, Barbara, happily accompanied her there. "At night we had dinner at the mayor's house. We sit down, I sit with the mayor and with everybody, all of the big shots because of my Uncle Benno. They knew who I was and everything because my uncle and my family were very well known." Jeannette and the other Holocaust survivors were treated very well by their hosts and she did not regret accepting the invitation to return to her hometown after having left there over 50 years before. "Then I had to speak German in front of school kids—they asked me to. They have a lot of Turkish people there, you know. And one girl says to me, 'I know what you felt, afterwards, because I don't feel wanted either sometimes here.'"

Like many Jews who had lost absolutely everything, Jeannette, only a few years earlier, had filed a lawsuit with the city of Cologne in order to try and recuperate her grandfather Josef Seligmann's family-owned land. "So I wrote to Germany, they can't find it, they can't find it. Then finally, when the statute of limitations was over, they found it. They built a golf course on it. They put a, like a suburb, they put a main highway through it. It was my grandfather's property." Jeannette's uncle, Arthur Marx, Salomon's brother who lived in hiding in Belgium, was successful in getting Salomon's insurance business office back at the cattle market. "He even put my father's name on the door again."[23] Arthur also returned to live in Cologne and, as stated previously, Uncle

Benno returned to Germany and helped reconstruct the country as set forth under the Marshall Plan. Initially, Jeannette was upset that Uncle Benno wanted to help reconstruct Germany. "I wasn't happy when I heard about it at first. When he helped them build it up then I realized he did the right thing."

Regarding her return trip to Cologne she states, "We stayed in a hotel right by the Cathedral in the middle of the city." Jeannette proudly displays a portrait of the Cologne Cathedral in her living room. When asked if she received an apology, she said, "They all apologized."

Jeannette enjoys being a grandmother and has been blessed with two highly accomplished grandsons, Adam and Joshua. The highlight for her is receiving their phone calls, thoughtful gifts in the mail, and visiting with them in person. Admittedly, Jeannette struggled for a long time with her faith. Like so many others, she could not understand, if there was a God, why He would allow an atrocity like the Holocaust to occur. "For a long time I didn't believe in God, but a friend of mine from India brought me back to my religion. He told me, 'Jeannette, *God didn't do it. It's what people did to people.*'" Once Jeannette realized where the blame appropriately fell, she made peace with this truth and peace with her Creator. Today, Jeannette is an active member of the Holocaust Survivors' Association and is often invited to share her story with students and other members of the public. "I thought, you know, because I wasn't in a concentration camp I wasn't a survivor but that doesn't go that way. I lost all my family and everything, you know."

Her philosophy today is, "I thank God everyday that I have a nice home, I don't owe anybody anything. 'Cause if you live on only what was, it's no good. Maybe that's why I'm still alive, I like to laugh. When you come from the Rhine, there's a different mentality, more laughter than tears."

Jeannette standing in front of the George Washington Bridge
April 13, 1947

Jeannette and Theodore Grunfeld

Jeannette on her return trip to Cologne, Germany, with her friend Barbara — 1993

March 2008

Dear Tracy,

I would like to Thank you very much, for writing the Book. I didn't realize that it would be such hard work. I was very impressed with your research into the Hitler & World War II years. I also learned a lot from your research and was greatly impressed by your information, from all the contacts you made, which I realized was very hard to achieve.

I got to respect you & love you as a good friend

Thank you again

Love Jeannette.

Now I will finish the book with my own thoughts. When I left home I was 17½ years old. I was very close to my parents. Thank God that loving parents, that made me who I am. Even in the worst of times my parents always taught me to think positively, that someone else has a bigger package to carry. My mother when you cry, you cry alone, but when you laugh, the world laughs with you. Always speak the truth, Do the best you can, also be there always to help others when you can. I tried to live the way I was taught & shown, by my parents deeds. I was very fortunate for the time I was with. I tried to teach those principles to Stephen & Bunny, my two children

Jeannette

Personal note of thanks from Jeannette

In Memoriam

Only guard yourself and guard your soul carefully, lest you forget the things your eyes saw, and lest these things depart your heart all the days of your life, and you shall make them known to your children, and to your children's children."

Deuteronomy 4:9

"My mother used to always tell me, "Laugh and the world laughs with you. When you cry, you cry alone." Jeannette had not yet joined the L.A.A.S when, unknown to her, the Nazis arrested her mother, Marianne, on October 29, 1941. Marianne arrived at the *Litzmannstadt* "Lodz" concentration camp on November 6, 1941. The last time Jeannette ever heard from her mother was ten months prior to her deportation, via Red Cross Geneva in December, 1940.[24] Fourteen other Marx/Seligmann family members were also arrested but it is not clear whether they were taken directly from Tante Hedwig's apartment house all at once or if they were forced to report to a central point of departure within days of each other. What is documented is that Tante Hedwig's address, 55 Wilhemstrasse, is the address given for all fifteen members, including two babies. Jeannette stated that her extended family "had nowhere else to live. They must have all moved in with Tante Hedwig."

As Jews were being deported between 1941 and '42, Jewish communities in the countryside of the Rhineland, where Salomon Marx' relatives resided, were extinguished. Only a small percentage were able to emigrate early enough.[25] Based on documented research,

Jeannette's relatives were deported separately to Riga, Lodz, and Minsk concentration camps.[26] On October 23, 1941, 2,014 Jews from Cologne, Germany, were deported to Litzmannstadt.

> Though there were no ghettos in Germany, Austria, Bohemia, and Luxembourg, the Jews there had come under the Nuremberg law for some time, their names and addresses were well-known and, beginning on September 19th, 1941, they wore Stars of David. Thus, after determining the total number of Jews anticipated for deportation in a given period, the Gestapo would either round them up or escort them to designated assembly points or have the offices of imposed Jewish organizations send out notices to the Jewish residents to report there on their own.[(1)] Between January 16, 1942, and May 15, 1942, large-scale genocide begins: 57,064 Jews from the Lodz ghetto (including 10,943 from Western Europe) are deported to the death camp at Chelmno. On August 23, 1944 there is a final transport from Lodz ghetto to Auschwitz; 700 Jews remain in the ghetto as a clean-up detail and 200 avoid deportation by hiding in the ghetto. By January 20th, 1945, 877 Jewish survivors in the ghetto are liberated by the Russian army.[(2)]

Due to conflicting information found in official records and other documentation, it is unclear whether Marianne perished in the Lodz ghetto, Chelmno, or elsewhere. Official index cards from the German Archives list Marianne as "missing," which appears to indicate the exact location and date of death went unrecorded. Rudi Billig's eyewitness account to Jeannette suggests he personally saw Marianne in Theresienstadt and that she was later deported to Auschwitz, where she was murdered.

Besides her priceless photographs, the only item left to physically link Jeannette to her parents and relatives forever is the *Poesie* album that her mother, Marianne, gave to her as a gift. To serve as an eternal remembrance and to honor Jeannette's family and friends, a description regarding each writer is included after his or her hand-written entry.

Between 1931 and 1939, before and during Hitler's rise to power, Jeannette requested family and friends write his or her own personal "poetry" entry for her. She later carried this special memento with her on the Kindertransport.(1)

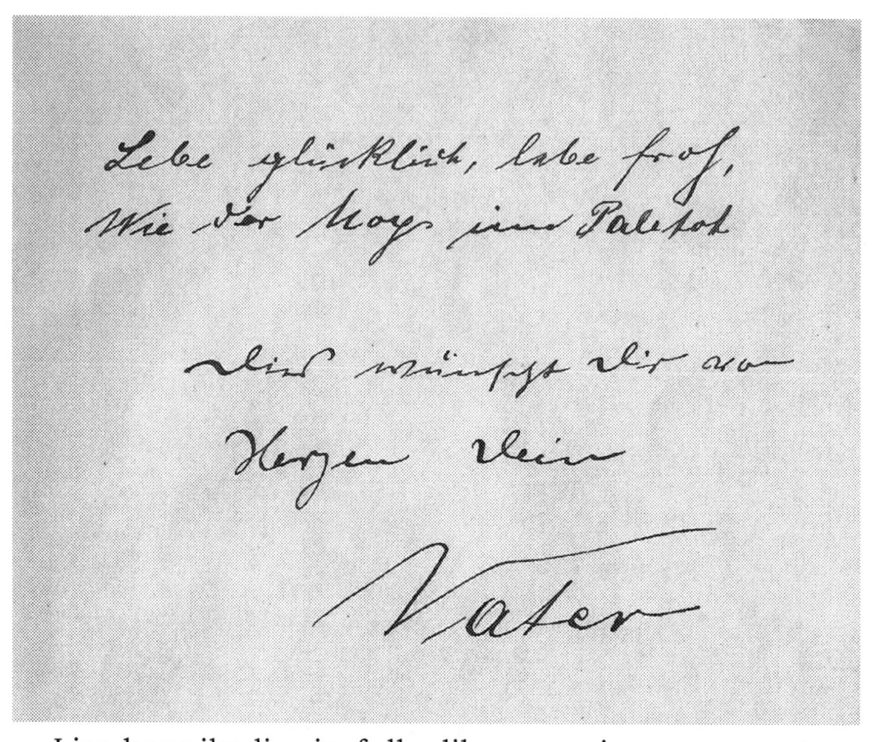

Lebe glücklich, lebe froh,
Wie der Mops im Paletot

Dies wünscht dir von
Herzen dein

Vater

Live happily, live joyfully, like a pug in an overcoat.

I'm wishing this for you with all of my heart.[27]

Your Father

Marx, Friedrich Salomon

Friedrich Salomon Marx was born in Weilerswist, Germany, in 1888. He was married to Marianne née *Seligmann. It is unknown how Salomon Marx perished. However, he was severely injured and left paralyzed as a result of the beatings he endured by Nazi sympathizers who assaulted him after he valiantly refused to relinquish his business. Salomon was not listed as one of the individuals taken from 55 Wilhelm Strasse. None of Jeannette's remaining family members told her exactly how her father died, although after her father's death, Jeannette received a letter from her cousin Kurt stating, "His last years were filled with so much pain, so that we must not begrudge this rest to him, and have to thank God for it." When Hanna Marx and Benedikt Marx returned to Germany after the war, they commissioned a gravestone for Salomon and Marianne in their honor.*

Jeannette with her father, Salomon

Salomon "Sally" Marx — July 23, 1888, to March 8, 1940
Marianne "Jenny" Marx née *Seligmann — Litzmannstadt 1942*

My parents' image appears in my eyes and so does their martyrdom
Through my eyes they smile and they cry
They guide me through all roads of my life
They continue to live — until my eyes close forever[28]

Aus Liebe!

Dir soll das Glück an jedem Morgen
Der Freude schönste Rosen streu'n
Und niemals sollen bange Sorgen
Beherrscher Deines Herzens sein!

Deine Dichliebende
Mutter!

14. 5. 32

With Love!
Each morning good luck shall spread
The most beautiful roses made from joy
And may anxious worries
Never rule your heart!

Your Mother loves you!
Mother!
14 February 1932

Marianne Marx

Marianne Marx née *Seligmann was born in Nippes in 1889 to Joseph and Jeannette. She was a housewife. Prior to WWII she lived in Köln, Germany. During the war she was in Köln, Germany. Marianne perished in Lodz, Poland. This information is based on a Page of Testimony submitted on 16 Aug 2002 by her researcher, a Shoah survivor.*(2) *Population registry books were kept by the Judenrat of the Łódź ghetto from the time of establishment of the Łódź Ghetto in February 1940 to just prior to its liquidation in August 1944. Records were maintained by apartment address, and were updated on a continuing basis. In addition to the names of the residents in an apartment, these records sometimes included the former addresses of the inhabitants, dates of birth, occupation, and date of deportation or death of the individual. In August 1944, the Nazis dissolved the Judenrat and the ghetto was liquidated. Thus, no entries were made about the fate of those deported to Auschwitz in the ghetto's last days.*(3)

Research indicates a Lodz Registry Book Entry for "Marjanne" Marx who was born July, 12th, 1889 in Köln (Cologne) Germany. The ghetto street she was assigned to was Runde Gasse and her living quarters were in 4 Flat 49. She appeared for registration on 12/06/42. No date of death for her is listed. Although the name is misspelled and day of her birth is slightly off, it is highly likely that the registered woman was Jeannette's mother, Marianne Marx. Two additional sources confirm she was transported to the Lodz ghetto. The following is a translation of an official Index Card recently released from German Archives.[29]

BA-17317

M A R X, Marianne 814 206

née Seligmann

Husband: Friedrich Salomon Jewish

7 July 1889 in Cologne German

29 October 1941 arrested in Cologne

Concentration Camp Lodz (Litzmannstadt)

Missing

A.f.Wg. Cologne[30] Str.[31]

Undated photo of Marianne with her daughter, Jeannette

In the moments of great sadness or those of joy[32]
I feel an anxiety to
Cry loud — and call:
Mother, do you see me, do you see me, Mother!
I do exist. I have survived.
I have grown up on my own.
I have abided by the principles
You implanted in me, I have built my family, my home
Have brought children to this world
And grandchildren you never saw …

Stolpersteine Memory Stone courtesy of Gunter Demnig[33]

אם אין אני לי מי לי?
וכשאני לעצמי מה אני
ואם לא עכשיו אמתי?

Wenn ich nicht für mich bin,
wer ist für mich?
Wenn ich nur für mich bin,
was bin ich?
Wenn nicht jetzt,
wann dann?

Religionsunterricht, letzte Stunde 1931

Abr. Reinhardt.

If I am not for myself,
Who is for me?
If I am for myself,
Who am I?
If not now
When?

Rabbi Reinhardt — 1931

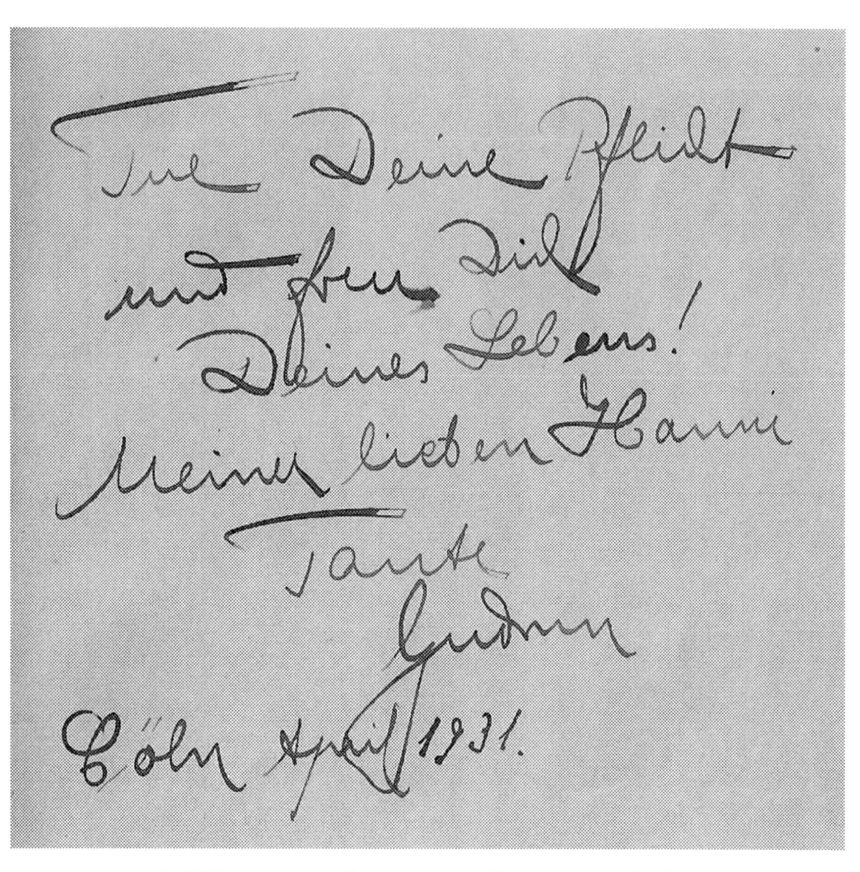

Tue Deine Pflicht
und freu Dich
Deines Lebens!
Meiner lieben Hanni
Tante
Gudrun
Cöln April 1931.

Fulfill your duty and enjoy life!

For my dear Hanni,

Aunt Gudrun

Cologne, April 1931

Marx, Gudrun

Gudrun Marx escaped with her husband, Benedikt, to London, England. Gudrun was a well-known dance performer in Germany. Although she had already retired by then, in September 1933 Nazi Joseph Goebbels took over the Chamber of Culture and excluded Jews from German cultural life, film, theater, music, fine arts, literature, and journalism.

GUDRUN HILDEBRANDT
mit ihren Meisterschülerinnen in ihrer Tanzdichtung „Wolken und Wind" nach Musik von Chopin

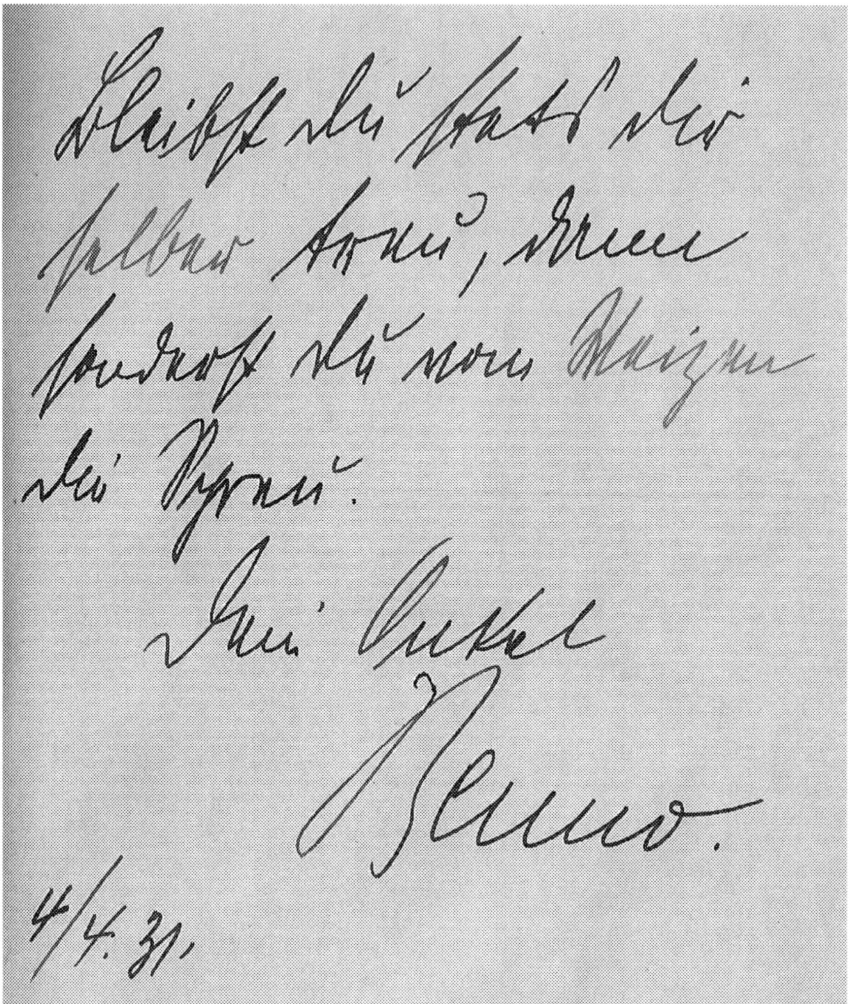
Bleibst du stets dir
selber treu, dann
trennst du vom Weizen
die Spreu.
Dein Onkel
Benno.
4/4. 31.

If you always remain true to yourself,

Then you separate the wheat from the chaff

Your Uncle Benno

4 April 1931

Marx, Benedikt

Benedikt Marx, a Social Democrat in the Reichstag, escaped Germany with his wife, Gudrun, to London. Benedikt left before Adolf Hitler was elected Chancellor. Benedikt went on to work for the British government during the War. As one of the councilors of the British Foreign Minister Bevin, he managed to convince him to reject the Morgenthau-Plan, which would have been unfavorable to Germany, and had been submitted by the American Secretary of the Treasury. Later, he assisted in formulating the Marshall Plan (European Recovery Program implemented in 1947) and returned to Germany to help rebuild his homeland.[4]

Undated photograph of Benedikt and Gudrun Marx

Undated photo of Uncle Benno and Tante Hanna

Zur Erinnerung!

Drei Engel mögen Dich
begleiten

Auf Deiner ganzen Lebensbahn

Und die drei Engel, die ich
meine

Sind: Liebe, Glück, Zufriedenheit.

Der lieben Hanni

von Ihrer

Cousine Ilse

Köln im März 1932

In Remembrance!

May three angels accompany you

During your entire life

And the three angels I'm thinking of

Are: Love, Happiness, and Contentment.

For dear Hanni

from her Cousin "Ilse"

Scheuer, Ilse

Ilse escaped Germany to England where she gained employment as a governess. Ilse now resides in Florida, and Jeannette and she remain in contact with one another.

Scheuer, Walter

Walter Scheuer was born in Sechtem in 1906 to Hermann and Bertha. He never married. Prior to WWII he lived in Weilerswist, Germany. During the war he was in Köln, Germany. Walter perished in the Shoah. This information is based on a Page of Testimony submitted on 18 Nov. 1998 by his researcher, a Shoah survivor.[(5)] Ilse's disabled brother, Walter, was several years older than Jeannette, although she remembers him. An eyewitness later provides testimony regarding the physical assault against Walter in his own hometown by the local chief of police and local Nazi sympathizers/members.[34] Walter was deported on December 6, 1941, from Cologne to Riga, where he perished.

Scheuer Bertha[35]

Mother of Ilse and Walter and sister of Marianne Seligmann

Bertha Scheuer née *Seligmann was born in Köln in 1880 to Joseph and Jeannette. She was married to Hermann. Prior to WWII she lived in Metternich, Germany. During the war she was in Köln, Germany. Bertha perished in Riga, Camp. This information is based on a Page of Testimony submitted on 03 Jun. 2002 by her researcher, a Shoah survivor.[(6)] Bertha was Marianne's oldest sister. It was at her wedding to Hermann where Marianne met Salomon for the first time.*

Scheuer, Hermann

Father of Ilse and Walter, husband to Bertha Scheuer

Herman Scheuer was born in 1840. Prior to WWII he lived in Weilerswist, Germany. Hermann perished in the Shoah. This information is based on a list of victims from Germany found in the Gedenkbuch-Opfer der Verfolgung der Juden unter der nationalsozialistischen Gewaltherrschaft in Deutschland 1933–1945, Bundesarchi*v (German National Archives), Koblenz 1986*

Ein Herz, das nie mit Wünschen
ruht,
Wird schwer sein Glück erringen
Wer gut u. treu das Seine tut,
Dem wird es Segen bringen!

Dies meine liebe Hanni von
Deiner Tante
Rosl.

Köln, 12. April 1931.

A heart that never stops wishing,

Will hardly achieve its happiness.

Whoever contributes well and faithfully,

Shall be blessed!

For my dear Hanni

From your Aunt Rosa.

Cologne, 12 April 1931

Marx, Rosa

Rosa was Salomon Marx' youngest sister. Tante Rosa married Sachar, a Latvian dentist. As life worsened under the Nazi regime, Sachar became desperate to get his family out of Germany. Because of Marianne's language skills, she accompanied Sachar to Holland to see the Consulate. The Consulate escorted Marianne and Sachar back to Germany to ensure he would not be deported to a concentration camp. Because he was a Latvian citizen, Sachar was allowed to take his wife, Rosa, and daughter, Sonja, to Riga with him. Rosa's governess willingly moved with the family. Sachar and Rosa fled to Russia when the Nazis took over Latvia. There, Sonja also became a dentist like her father.

Once the war was over, the family returned to Germany. To their great surprise they learned that the fair, young governess who so willingly moved with the family to Latvia, was actually spying for the Nazis.

Sonja resides in Israel and she and Jeannette still keep in touch.

Wie sich Dein Leben wendet,

Wie oft Dich's quält, wie oft
Dir's lacht,

Die Zeit war nie verschwendet

In der Du jemand froh gemacht.

Zur steten Erinnerung
an Deine Tante
Paula.

Köln. Nippes
4. I. 39.

No matter how our life turns out,
How often it torments you, or
How often it smiles on you,
The time was never wasted
Whenever you have used it
To make someone happy.
In eternal memory of your Aunt Paula.

Cologne-Nippes
4 January 1939

Seligmann, Paula

Paula Seligmann née *Greif was born in Hesse, Germany, in 1891 to Gutkind and Biena. She was a housewife. Prior to WWII she lived in Köln, Germany. During the war she was in Köln, Germany. Paula perished in Riga, Camp. This information is based on a Page of Testimony submitted on 12 Aug. 2000 by her researcher, a Shoah survivor.*(7)

According to Rudi's letter to Jeannette, Paula died of sickness while in Riga.

Acht' den Armen wie den Reichen

Tue redlich Deine Pflicht.

Jeder Mensch ist Deinesgleichen,

Drum vor Menschen beug Dich nicht!

Dir, lb. Hanni, zur Beherzigung

und Erinnerung

5. 1. 1939

an Deinen Vetter

Otto.

Respect the poor just as the rich

And fulfill your duty in honesty.

Every human is just like you,

Therefore don't bow down before men!

For you, dear Hanni, to take to heart,

and to remember your Cousin Otto.

5 January 1939

Seligmann, Otto

Otto was born in 1926 and deported in 1941 to Riga along with his mother, Paula, and sister, Ine. He was just fifteen years old.[8]

In his letter to Jeannette, Rudi states as an eyewitness that Otto "died at the Riga Ghetto from a disease."

Mach Gehorsam Dir zu eigen,
Folge gern der Mutter Wort;
Lerne hören, lerne schweigen,
Aber stets am rechten Ort!

Zur stetem Erinnerung
an Deine Cousine
Ine.

Köln-Nippes, den 5. Jan. 1939

Acquire obedience,
Gladly follow your mother's advice;
Learn to listen, learn to hold your tongue,

But each at all times in the right place!

To always remember

your Cousin Ine

Cologne-Nippes, January 5th, 1939

Seligmann, Ine

Current research has failed to produce documentation regarding Ine's fate. Rudi Billig, however, in his letter to Jeannette, mentions Ine in Riga: "… and Ine was present in one of the many or 'usual' actions at the end of 1943." Rudi was possibly referring to documented Jewish resistance fighters and the uprisings that occurred against their Nazi captors in Riga at the time.[36]

Lieber Hannes

Wenn Du einst als Großmama
im Lehnstuhl sitzt bei Großpapa
So denke oft mit heiteren Blick,
An Deine Freundin Jolly zurück.

Vergesse mich nicht
ich tue's auch nicht

Zum ewigen Andenken an Deine
Jolly.

1.1.1939

Dear Hannes,

When you once as Grandmama
Sit in a recliner next to Grandpapa,
Remember often and cheerfully,
Your girl friend Jolly.

Don't forget me, I won't forget you either.
In eternal remembrance of your Jolly
1 January 1939

"Jolly" is on the left. Jeannette is on the right and "Mops" is in the middle. It is unknown whether these classmates and close friends of Jeannette escaped the Holocaust.

1. 1. 1939.

Lieber Hannes.
Denk noch oft an mich,
wie ich an Dich,
an die Vorlehrezeit
in der wir manch frohe Stunde
verlebt,
Stunden die ich Dir auch auf
deinen fernen Lebensweg
wünsche.

Dein Mops.

Dear Hannes, *1 January 1939*

Think of me often,

Just as I think of you

Back to the time before our apprenticeship

When we spent many a happy hour together,

Such hours I wish for you

During your distant path in life as well.

Your Pug *"Mops"*

Willst du glücklich sein auf
Erden,
Trage bei zu andrer Glück;
Denn die Freude, die wir
geben,
Kehrt ins eigne Herz zurück.

Dies schrieb dir l. Hanni zur
freundl. Erinnerung

Frau Falkenstein

Köln-Nippes den 12.3.34.

If you want to be happy on earth,
Contribute to the happiness of others;
Since the joy that we extend,
Returns into our own heart.
This was written for you, dear Hanni,
in kind remembrance by
Mrs. Falkenstein
Cologne-Nippes, March 12th, 1934

Mrs. Falkenstein was the poor neighbor that Salomon Marx faithfully brought fresh beef to each Friday from the cattle market.

Köln den 3. Januar 1939

Freundschaft!

Gar freundliche Gesellschaft
leistet uns

Ein fern ferner Freund, wenn wir ihn
glücklich wissen.

Ach, in der Ferne zeigt sich alles
reiner,

Was in der Gegenwart uns nur
verwirrt!

Vielleicht wirst du erkennen, welche
Liebe

Dich überall umgab, und welchen
Wert

Die Treue wahrer Freundschaft hat,
und wie

Die weite Welt die Nächsten nicht
ersetzt.

Gewidmet in treue Freundschaft

Luise

Cologne, January 3rd, 1939

Friendship!

A friend who is far away,

Of whom we know that he is happy,

Is very good company to us.

Oh, how everything looks clearer when distant,

While it confuses us while present!

Perhaps you will recognize, how surrounded by

Love

You were everywhere, and how valuable

The faithfulness of true friendship, and how

The world far and wide, does not replace

Those who are closest.

Dedicated in true friendship

Luise

Luise is the Christian friend who, after Jeannette left, continued shopping for her parents and bringing the food over in the middle of the night to avoid Nazi detection and arrest.

23. 3. 31.

Im Handeln immer treu und wahr!
Im Reden immer schlicht und klar!
In dem, was du versprichst, getreu!
Das deines Lebens Richtschnur sei!

Der lieben Hanni
von ihrer 1. Lehrerin
Hanna Hengelberg.

23 March 1931

May your actions always be faithful and true!

May your speech be responsible and clear!

Whatever you promise, faithfully keep!

May this be the guideline in your life!

To dear Hanni

from her teacher

Hanna Mengelberg

Mengelberg, Hanna

It is unknown whether Ms. Mengelberg, Jeannette's first school teacher, escaped the Holocaust.

Köln-Nipps 4. März 34.

Souvenir!

Lerne leiden ohne klagen
Lerne dulden und entsagen
Lern vergessen und vergeben
Und du hast gelernt zu
leben.

Dies schrieb Dir
Dein Vetter
Werner

Koln-Nippes 4 March 34

Souvenir!
Learn to suffer without complaining
Learn to endure
And forbearance
Learn to forget and to forgive
Then you have learned to live

Written for you by
Your Cousin Werner

Undated photo of Jeannette's cousin Werner

Seligmann, Werner

Werner escaped Nazi Germany by migrating to the United States. His mother Paula's family members sponsored him and he was able to obtain a visa. Wanting to leave the past behind and begin a new life as a U.S. citizen, Werner changed his name to "Alfred Shaw." He helped facilitate Jeannette's migration to the U.S.

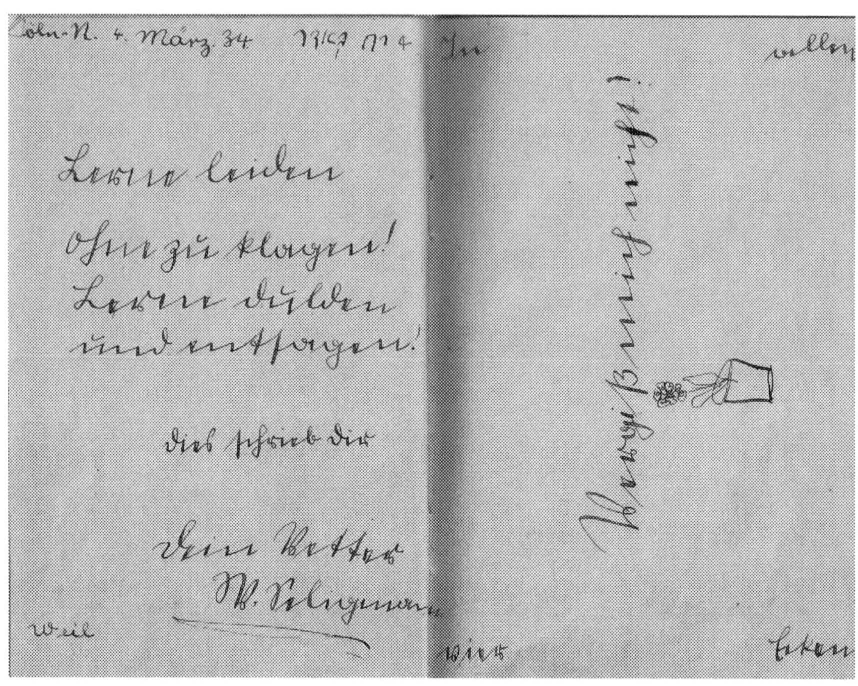
Köln-N. 4. März 34

Lerne leiden

Ohne zu klagen!
Lerne dulden
und entsagen!

Dies schreibt dir

Dein Vetter
W. Seligmann

Weil

In allen vier Ecken

Vergißmeinnicht!

Cologne-N. 4. March 1934

חי

רזאב

Learn to suffer

Without complaining!

Learn to endure

And forbearance!

Written for you by

Your Cousin

(OTTO) W. Seligmann

Weil

In all four corners Forget-Me-Not!

Seligmann, Otto

Otto was Marianne's older brother and the two were very close because they were only five years apart in age. Jeannette recalls at one point that her uncle Otto asked Jeannette's parents if he could take her to South Africa with him and his second wife. Otto considered starting an oil business there as life grew unbearable in Germany. For unknown reasons, this plan never transpired. Otto and his wife took their own lives rather than face the horrors that awaited them at the hands of the Nazis. Suicide under the Nazi regime was not uncommon as Jews, in complete and utter despair, saw this as their only way of escaping a hopeless situation.

Seligmann, Arthur

Currently, there are no known records documenting Arthur Seligmann's fate. However, it is believed he perished in the Holocaust. Jeannette recounts that Arthur and his wife, Emilie, had a son, Kurt, who was well established in the United States. In fact, he co-owned a uniform factory in Alabama. The factory was started by Emilie's brother and sister. Both Kurt and his aunt and uncle sponsored Arthur and Emilie for entry into the United States. Arthur and Emilie had already obtained their passports and visas. The two traveled to Holland where they waited to receive their permit for entry into the United States. To their shock and disbelief, the U.S. refused them entry. As a result, the couple was deported from Holland to Auschwitz, where they perished.

Seligmann, Emilie

Emilie Seligmann née *Kahn was born in Bockenheim in 1877 to Julius and Regine. She was a housewife and married to Arthur. Prior to WWII she lived in Köln, Germany. During the war she was in Köln, Germany. Emilie perished in Auschwitz, Camp. This information is based on a Page of Testimony submitted on 21 Jul. 2000 by her researcher, a Shoah survivor.*[9]

Zur Erinnerung!

Die Welt dieß ist ein Schauspiel-
haus, das Schicksal teilt die Rollen aus.
Wohl dem, der seine Rolle so gespielt
daß wenn der Vorhang fällt,
ihn keine Reue fühlt!

Meiner l. Nichte Hanni zum
steten Gedenken an Ihre
Mamatante Hedwig.

Köln-Nippes den 4. 1. 1939

In Remembrance!

The world is a theatre play,

Louse, the fate, distributes the roles.

After the curtain falls, lucky the one, who,

After having played his role, did it

In such a way that he does not feel remorse!

For my dear niece Hanni, to

always remember her maternal Aunt Hedwig.

Cologne-Nippes, January 4th, 1939

Freund, Hedwig

Hedwig Freund née *Seligmann was born in Köln in 1881 to Joseph and Janette. She was a housewife and married to Julius. Prior to WWII she lived in Rhoden, Germany. During the war she was in Köln, Germany. Hedwig perished in Minsk, Camp (USSR). Submitted on 06 Jun. 2002 by her researcher, a Shoah survivor.*[10]

Jeannette greatly loved Marianne's older sister, Hedwig, because she lived nearby and they saw each other regularly. "She was like a mother to me." Records indicate that Hedwig and her husband, Julius, took in several Marx/Seligmann family members when they had nowhere else to escape.

December 12, 1937, photo of Aunt Hedwig

HIER WOHNTE
HEDWIG
FREUND
GEB. SELIGMANN
JG. 1881
DEPORTIERT 1941
ŁODZ
FÜR TOT ERKLÄRT

Freund, Julius

Julius Freund was born in Rhoden in 1880 to Wolf and Pienchen. He was married to Hedwig née *Seligmann. Prior to WWII he lived in Rhoden, Germany, then moved to Köln, Germany, where he resided with his wife, Hedwig, at #55 Wilhelmstrasse. The couple lived just a few houses away from Salomon and Marianne Marx. It appears they sheltered many Marx/Seligmann family members before they, along with these members, were deported to the ghettos. Julius perished in Minsk, Belorussia (USSR). This information is based on a Page of Testimony submitted on 15 Sep. 1999 by his researcher, a Shoah survivor.*[(11)]

This information is based on a list of victims from Germany found in the Gedenkbuch - Opfer der Verfolgung der Juden unter der nationalsozialistischen Gewaltherrschaft in Deutschland 1933–1945, Bundesarchiv *(German National Archives), Koblenz 1986.*

Further research indicates a Lodz Registry Book Entry of "Julius Freund" from Köln (Cologne), Germany. The ghetto street Julius was assigned to was Richter Strasse and his living quarters were in 9 Flat 28. Julius and Hedwig were presumably transported from the Lodz ghetto to Minsk camp where they perished. Julius died on 10/04/43.

Undated photo of Uncle Julius

HIER WOHNTE
JULIUS
FREUND
JG. 1880
DEPORTIERT 1941
ŁODZ
FÜR TOT ERKLÄRT

It was from Unkle Julius' and Tante Hedwig's home at 55 Wilhelmstrasse that Jeannette left for Kindertransport. This home was also the place where 15 of Jeannette's family members (including her own mother) were arrested by the Gestapo then deported to their deaths.

Present-day photograph of Seligmann/Marx Stolperstines in front of 55 Wilhelmstrasse — Courtesy of artist Gunter Demnig

Present-day photograph of the Stolpersteines representing fifteen Marx and Seligmann family members who perished in the Holocaust

Courtesy of artist Gunter Demnig

Author's Note

During a 2004 family vacation to Washington D.C., I visited the United States Holocaust Memorial Museum. My experience touring the museum was unforgettable. The first exhibit I saw was a striped blue and grey jacket formerly worn by a concentration camp prisoner. As I gazed at the woven material with its pale-blue dyed stripes, I thought about the person who wore it and the unspeakable suffering this jacket represented. I later made my way towards an old wooden boxcar on display and stepped inside. This boxcar, originally intended for transporting livestock, was instead used for human cargo. I will never forget the smell. The odor is virtually impossible to describe: a faint mixture of old, musty wood along with images in my mind of countless individuals packed in so tightly with one another they could hardly breathe. I could practically hear their sobs and cries of loss and confusion. Within the quiet darkness of that empty wooden boxcar, all of my senses were consumed with overwhelming sadness.

Stepping out, I continued to make my way through the exhibits and stopped to view a display case that held the actual instruments, charts, and hair-strand color samples used under the Nazi regime to determine whether or not a person was *Aryan*. The instruments measured nose length, the charts determined eye color, and the hair-strand samples determined the degree of darkness of a person's hair. There were black-and-white photos showing children being inhumanely tested like animals. There, next to the *Euthanasia* display, was another black-and-white photograph of a lonely little girl staring into the camera. This very normal-looking child was deemed mentally disabled and the photograph of her was taken just before she was euthanized. She was one of the countless children who were killed under the Nazi euthanasia program.

As we remember the horrors that took place during the Holocaust, a common cry is, "Never again!" We are appalled by the genocide that continues to take place in regions like Darfur as well as the rampant human rights violations in countries such as China. Yet in the not so distant past, an industrialized, civilized society was swayed by a tract called *Permissions for the Destruction of Life Unworthy of Life.* This tract, written in 1920 by highly respected German professors Alfred Hoche and Karl Binding, led to the eventual acceptance of *Aktion T-4*, the Nazi Euthanasia ("good death") program.[(1)]

I would later learn that one of the first victims of the Holocaust was an infant referred to in history books as "Baby Knauer." Apparently, the baby's father wrote to Adolf Hitler asking that his son be "put to sleep." Baby Knauer was born blind, and missing a leg and part of an arm. Hitler sent one of his personal physicians to verify the child's disabilities and, once confirmed, gave his consent for the baby to be euthanized without legal repercussions. Hitler eventually signed a secret decree allowing disabled infants to be legally euthanized.[(2)] After the "mercy killing" of baby Knauer, came the eventual 1939 order for midwives and doctors to report for registration disabled newborns and children up to three years of age. Serious diseases that midwives and doctors were ordered to report included "idiocy, mongolism, microcephaly, hydrocephaly, paralysis, and spastic conditions and malformations of all kinds, but especially of the limbs, head and spinal column." The killings were carried out in institutions and the criteria eventually grew to include even minor disabilities. Youths considered to be juvenile delinquents were included as well. Jewish children were included in the euthanasia program simply for being Jewish.[(3)] When an inmate asked S.S. Doctor Fritz Klein how he reconciled the deaths taking place in Auschwitz with the physician's Hippocratic Oath to preserve life, he replied, "Of course I am a doctor and I want to preserve life, and out of respect for human life, I would remove a gangrenous appendix from a diseased body. The Jew is the gangrenous appendix in the body of mankind."[(4)]

Undoubtedly, *eugenics*, a word coined by Francis Galton (Charles Darwin's cousin) meaning "well born," played a major role in the destruction of Jewish lives as well as the murders of the disabled and elderly: lives unworthy of life. Jews were considered *racially inferior* and the physically and mentally disabled were *weak and defective*. Keeping the *undesirables* alive in institutions and through medical assistance only disrupted the natural selection process.(5) This is the exhibit where I learned for the first time about my own country's culpability in regard to eugenics ideology. In 1907, the United States implemented its first compulsory sterilization law based on eugenics, and by 1924, 3,000 people had been forcibly sterilized. Up through the mid-1970s, over 60,000 U.S. citizens had been forcibly sterilized.(6) Among other eugenics proponents at the time was Planned Parenthood founder Margaret Sanger, who stated in her 1922 book *The Pivot of Civilization:*

> Every single case of inherited defect, every malformed child, every congenitally tainted human being brought into this world is of infinite importance to that poor individual; but it is of scarcely less importance to the rest of us and to all of our children who must pay in one way or another for these biological and racial mistakes. (7)

Sanger also stated in her 1920 book *Woman and the New Race* (published by Eugenics Publishing Company, NY):

> No more children should be born when the parents, though healthy themselves, find that their children are physically or mentally defective. No matter how much they desire children, no man and woman have a right to bring into the world those who are to suffer from mental or physical affliction. It condemns the child to a life of misery and places upon the community the burden of caring for it, probably for its defective descendants for many generations.(8)

In *Mein Kampf*, written in 1925, Adolf Hitler stated:

> In opposition to [Marxism], the volkish philosophy finds the importance of mankind in its basic racial elements. In the state it sees no principle only a means to an end and construes its end as a preservation of the racial existence of man. Thus it by no means

> believes in the equality of the races, but along with their differences it recognizes their higher or lesser value and feels itself obligated, through this knowledge, to promote the victory of the better and stronger, and demand the subordination of the inferior and weaker in accordance with the eternal will that dominates this universe.[9]

The reason I found the euthanasia exhibit so utterly disturbing is because the act is clearly being carried out today by some within the medical community under the banner of "mercy." What started out as requests by *consenting* terminally ill adults to be given the right to die has now given way to non-consenting babies being euthanized. Common sense would indicate that programs euthanizing newborns today could very well include toddlers, elementary school children, and teenagers tomorrow.

On March 10, 2005, *The New England Journal of Medicine* published an article by Eduard Verhagen, M.D., J.D., and Pieter J.J. Sauer, M.D., Ph.D. entitled "The Groningen Protocol-Euthanasia in Severely Ill Newborns." This article sets forth a list of standards for euthanizing newborns with serious and incurable deformities. The following is an excerpt from that article:

> . . . the national survey indicated that such procedures are performed in 15 to 20 newborns per year, the fact that an average of three cases were reported annually suggests that most cases are simply not being reported. We believe that all cases must be reported if the country is to prevent uncontrolled and unjustified euthanasia and if we are to discuss the issue publicly and thus further develop norms regarding euthanasia in newborns.[10]

The article states that many of these babies suffered from extreme forms of spina bifida. In 1999, at Vanderbilt University Medical Center, 21-week old "Baby Samuel" underwent successful corrective spina bifida surgery in utero.

In response to the Groningen Protocol, Dr. Alan B. Jotkowitz, Department of Medicine, Faculty of Health Sciences, Ben-Gurion University of the Negev, Israel, had this to say:

> The Groningen protocol allows for the euthanasia of severely ill newborns with a hopeless prognosis and unbearable suffering.

> We understand the impetus for such a protocol but have moral and ethical concerns with it. Advocates for euthanasia in adults have relied on the concept of human autonomy, which is lacking in the case of infants. In addition, biases can potentially influence the decision making of both parents and physicians. It is also very difficult to weigh the element of quality of life on the will to live. We feel an important line has been crossed if the international medical community consents to the active euthanasia of severely ill infants and are concerned about the extension of the policy to other at risk groups.[11]

Finally, notable Princeton University Professor, Peter Singer was asked this question on his website: "You have been quoted as saying: 'Killing a defective infant is not morally equivalent to killing a person. Sometimes it is not wrong at all.' Is that quote accurate?"

His response:

> It is accurate, but can be misleading if read without an understanding of what I mean by the term "person" (which is discussed in *Practical Ethics*, from which that quotation is taken). I use the term "person" to refer to a being who is capable of anticipating the future, of having wants and desires for the future. As I have said in answer to the previous question, I think that it is generally a greater wrong to kill such a being than it is to kill a being that has no sense of existing over time. Newborn human babies have no sense of their own existence over time. So killing a newborn baby is never equivalent to killing a person, that is, a being who wants to go on living. That doesn't mean that it is not almost always a terrible thing to do. It is, but that is because most infants are loved and cherished by their parents, and to kill an infant is usually to do a great wrong to its parents.[12]

Those human beings responsible for carrying out untold atrocities against other humans have not been the physically disabled or those with mental disabilities such as Down syndrome. They are people such as Adolf Hitler, who had the very strong allegiance of highly educated professors, lawyers, physicians and other elites. They are powerful individuals such as former Yugoslav President Slobodan Milosevic, who studied law and became a successful businessman and banker before becoming president and committing large-scale genocidal atrocities. There are no genetics tests to determine which child will eventually grow up to become another Hitler, Pol Pot, or Stalin. Even if there were, those tests would be far from infallible as healthy babies have sometimes been mistakenly diagnosed as "disabled." What I learned during my visit to the USHMM is that we must be a voice for the weak and speak up for those individuals and groups who cannot defend themselves.

The exhibit that visually impacted me the most was the shoe display. There they were, a countless sea of shoes piled on top of each other. Men's dress shoes, women's high heels, children's shoes, and toddler shoes among many, many others. This visually powerful combination of shoes represented men, women, children, and babies who were stripped of their dignity and completely dehumanized. Their shoes survived but the people who once wore them were impenitently destroyed. Directly above the shoe display is this poem:

Moishe Shulstein
I Saw a Mountain
We are the shoes, we are the last witnesses.
We are shoes from grandchildren and grandfathers,
From Prague, Paris and Amsterdam,
And because we are only made of fabric and leather
And not of blood and flesh, each one of us avoided the hellfire.

As I passed through The Hall of Remembrance, I stopped to read its walls:

I call heaven and earth to witness this day: I have put before you life and death, blessing and curse. Choose life — that you and your offspring shall live.

Deuteronomy 30:19

Taking a moment to light a candle in this luminous white room, I said a short prayer and reflected on these final words:

First they came for the Jews
and I did not speak out
because I was not a Jew.
Then they came for the Communists
and I did not speak out
because I was not a Communist.
Then they came for the trade unionists
and I did not speak out
because I was not a trade unionist.
Then they came for me
and there was no one left
to speak out for me.

Pastor Martin Niemöller I

Thank you, Jeannette, for showing me how a beautiful soul can rise out of the ashes of tragedy and go on to make such an unforgettable impact on the lives of others.

Your eternal friend,

Tracy

"There is no pit so deep that God's love is not deeper still."

Corrie ten Boom—Holocaust survivor whose family hid persecuted Jews in their home in Holland.

APPENDIX

- Jeannette Marx' Family Lineage
- Michael Marx' Gravestone
- Translation of Michael Marx Gravestone
- Walter Scheuer Testimony
- Translation of Jeannette's Birth Certificate
- English Translation of *Kindertransport* List of Personal Items
- Hand-Written letter from Jeannette's parents
- Letter from Jeannette's Cousin Kurt
- London Auxiliary Ambulance Service Certificate of Training
- Rare World War II London Auxiliary Ambulance Service Postcards by artist "SAX."
- Disbandment of the Civil Defence Services letter to Jeannette Marx
- Appreciation letter from the London County Council to all who served during wartime
- Arthur Marx' "Loss of German Citizenship" Document
- 1942 Notice to Cologne Jews from the Jewish Religious Federation
- Deportations and the Ghettos
- Stolpersteine Memorial
- Corrected Copy of Marianne Marx' Birth Certificate

Marx Family Lineage[37]

Andreas Kahn or Cahen[38] Family and Sibilla Arend or Aaron

Andreas Kahn, Cahen (Jeannette's paternal great-great-great grandfather) was born about 1749 and resided in Klein Vernich, Germany. He married Sibilla Arend (Aaron) about 1784 and made a living as a butcher and merchant. Andreas died on 01/17/1802 in Klein Vernich. Since there was no official guide for German spelling at the time, names were simply spelled as the scribe heard them.

Marriage records indicate Sibilla married Adolph Marx sometime after the death of her husband Andreas. Sibilla and Andreas' children adopted their step-father's last name of "Marx." The surname Marx was also an approved "German sounding" surname and Jews with last names that sounded too "Jewish" were required by legislation to change them and to adopt an approved "German" surname.

Sibilla had the following children:

Gudula Marx (Cahen)
Born: about 1783 in Vernich

Michael Marx (Cahen) - (Jeannette's great-great grandfather)
Born: 1790 in Vernich, who later became a merchant

Eva Marx
Born: about 1795 in Vernich

Aaron Marx (Cahen)
Born: No records available

Philipp Marx (Cahen), *merchant in Weilerswist and founder of* *the synagogue of Weilerswist.*

Born: about 1797
Died: 17 April 1874

In 1774 there were four Jewish families in Weilerswist, among them also a Leiser Cain from Kerpen, butcher by profession, and married to Eva Arens (marriage about 1772). Their children used the name Katz after 1808. Eva Arens is the sister of Sibilla Arend, the wife of Andreas Kahn from Vernich.

At the Jewish cemetery in Walberberg is a gravestone with the following inscription:

Rabbi Moshe Jechiel haKohen died in the year 616. That is Michael Katz from Weilerswist:

Born: 1784 in Weilerswist
Died: 1856 in Walberberg

Michael Marx Family and Rosa Baruch

Michael Marx, (Jeannette's great-great grandfather) son of Andreas Cahn and Sibilla Arend, became a Jewish merchant in Vernich in 1818, a merchant in Metternich in 1836, and a butcher in Metternich 1839. On March 25th, 1818, he married Rosa (Röschen) Baruch (b. 1796 In Oberbieber). Philipp Marx, a "peddler from Vernich" and Weilerswist synagogue founder was listed as a witness to the marriage.

Michael and Rosa's Children:

Andreas Marx
Born: 25 November 1818

Remark: Andreas married Sibilla Schüler on 06/12/1844. On Andreas Marx' gravestone is the following description: Asher ben Jechiel ha-Kohen and depicted on the gravestone are priestly hands and crown. On his wife Sibilla's gravestone is this description: Shlomo ha-Levi. They had a daughter, Regina, who was born in 1848. [39]

Bernhard Marx
Born: 8 August 1820

Arnoldus Marx
Born: 22 December 1822

Hermann Marx (Jeannette's great-grandfather).
Born: 7 June 1825
Death Certificate: 34/1909

Helena Marx
Born: 26 July 1827

Gudula Marx
Born: 6 November 1830

Mauriz (Moses) Marx
Married to Maria Anna Marx, daughter of Philipp Marx and Sibilla Horn
Born: 9 March 1832
Died: 23 April 1864 in Groß-Vernich

Leopold Marx
Born: 4 December 1833

Sybilla Marx
Born: 15 October 1836
Friederich Wilhelm Marx
Born: 7 March 1839

Hermann Marx Family and Sara (Anna) Wolf [40]

Hermann Marx was born on June 7, 1825, and married Sara Wolf on May 1, 1850. He was a butcher in Weilerswist in 1856 and a merchant in Weilerswist in 1866. Hermann died on July 30, 1909.

Wife: Sara Wolf
Born: 7 November 1826 in Ochtendung
Died: 23 April 1881 in Weilerswist

Children:

Carl Marx
Born: 21 November 1854 in Hersel
Died: 2 December 1858 in Hersel

Michael Marx (Jeannette's paternal grandfather).
Born: 5 November 1856

Michael Marx was born on November 5, 1856. He married Franzisca Nussbaum on August 17th, 1887. Witnesses at the marriage were Hermann Marx (father) and Michael Marx (great-grandfather).

Remark: Franzisca "Fannie" Nussbaum (Jeannette's paternal grandmother) was born on October 28th, 1857 in Weimarschmieden. Franzisca died on June 4, 1928. Jeannette recalls her grandmother "Fannie" was staying with Jeannette's family in Cologne. Fannie gave Jeannette a gift for her 7th birthday that morning and when Jeannette returned home from school, she learned that her grandmother had passed away.

Helena Marx, *married to Andreas Kossmann, born 3 November 1861, died on 10 November 1920 in Weilerswist*

Born: 12 June 1859
Marriage: 18 October 1887
Died: 6 May 1913 in Weilerswist

Benedikt Marx, married to Lina Kaufmann
Born: 19 September 1863
Remark: At Benedikt's birth witnesses were Andreas Marx, who was born in 1818, butcher from Wesseling; and Abraham Carl, butcher in Weilerswist.

Rosa Marx
Born: 4 July 1866

Eva Marx
Born: 30 March 1869
Died: 16 June 1877

Michael Marx Family and Franzisca Nussbaum[41]

Children:

****Friedrich Salomon Marx (Jeannette's Father).***
Born: 23 July 1888
Birth Certificate: 61/1888
Died: 19 March 1941 in Köln Ehrenfeld
Death Certificate: 286/1941 Köln Ehrenfeld

Benedict Marx, married to Gudrun Hildebrand from Berlin
Born: 10 October 1889
Died: 27 October 1956 in Bad Godesberg

Remark: Benedikt (Uncle Benno) was known to Jeannette as "Benjamin." Uncle Benno married Gudrun Hildebrand (German, mixed marriage) and they had no children. Benedict Marx held a vital role in the reconstruction of Germany after World War II ended.

Max Marx
Born: 22 February 1896
Died: 1906

Arthur Marx
Born: 1900
Died: 20 October 1962 in Köln Lindenthal

Johanna Marx
Born: 23 January 1891
Remark: Jeannette referred to Johanna Marx as "Tante Hanna." Tante Hanna escaped to England and assisted Jeannette when she arrived on the Kindertransport. After the war ended, Tante Hanna moved to the United States and lived with Jeannette and her family. Johanna Marx never married and had no children.

Caroline Marx
Born: 8 December 1892
Remark: Caroline was known to Jeannette as "Lina." She apparently died of an illness sometime before Jeannette was born.

Rosa Marx
Born: 20 May 1894
Remark: Rosa married "Sachar" and they had one child, Sonja.

Isaak Scheuer Family and Gudula Marx[42]

Isaak Scheuer was a butcher in Metternich in 1869 and a merchant in Metternich in 1871. He was born in 1839 in Poppelsdorf and married Gudula Marx, the daughter of Michael Marx and Rosa Baruch (Jeannette's great-great grandparents). Isaak died on March 13, 1915 in Metternich. One of their sons was Hermann Scheuer.

Hermann Scheuer Family and Bertha Seligmann

Hermann Scheuer was born on April 4, 1873. He resided In Weilerswist and made his living as a cattle merchant and owner of a manufactured goods shop. Hermann married Bertha Seligmann, the daughter of Josef

Seligmann (Jeannette's maternal grandfather). Hermann and Bertha were deported on December 6, 1941, from Cologne to Riga.

Remark: Jeannette's father, Salomon Marx, was Hermann Scheuer's cousin. Salomon was first introduced to Jeannette's mother, Marianne Seligmann at Hermann Scheuer's wedding to Bertha Seligmann, Marianne's older sister.

Josef Seligmann and Jeannette Kahn are Marianne's parents. Josef resided with Jeannette in Cologne, Germany. He was a successful merchant and co-founder of the *Glockengasse Synagogue*. Their children were Hedwig, Bertha, Sigmund, Arthur, Julius, Otto, and Marianne. Marianne was the youngest and she was born in Cologne on July 13th, 1889.

Hermann and Bertha Scheuer had five children:

Hildegard Jeannette Scheuer*, married to Ludwig Graebner from Frankfurt in 1933 (co-owner of the Terranova Factory), died 1980 in Holland.* [43]

Born: 1905 in Sechtem
Died: 30 May 1975 in Holland

Walter Scheuer (Disabled)
Born: 6 March 1909 in Weilerswist
Died: Deported on 06 December 1941 from Cologne to Riga

Martha Scheuer
Born: 1 February 1909 in Weilerswist
Died: 17 March 1911 in Weilerswist

Henrietta Scheuer
Born: 3 June 1914 in Weilerswist
Birth Certificate: 42/1914

Ilse Scheuer, married to Mr. Enrick, Florida
Born: 2 December 1915 in Weilerswist
Birth Certificate: 74/1915
Remark: Emigrated to England in mid 1930

Grave Stone of Michael Marx [44]

30

Front:

Here is buried
A man, honest and upright, who walked with integrity
and did justice, he was pious all of his days
a righteous man who lived by his faith
This is Jechiel, son of Asher Ka'z from the village of
Metternich, who died in good old age
and was buried on 14 Schewat
With a good reputation on the fifteenth of the year
616 according to small count
May his soul be bound up in the bond of eternal life

Back:

Michael Marx
from Metternich

Testimony of Walter Scheuer Assault

I knew that back then, Jews were transported from our local district to Cologne. Among them was also the mentally challenged[45] Walter Scheuer. One day I only heard that Walter Scheuer had returned and was staying with Mrs. —. — also lived at the Triftstrasse. At the same time I was told that the police had already arrested Scheuer again, and so I watched at the Graberstrasse when the police officer was leading Scheuer away. But — was not alone, I also saw — who was lending — a hand. Walter Scheuer was screaming something terrible. xxxxxxxxxxxxxxxxxxxxxxxxxxxxxxxxxxxxxxxx

xxxxxxxxxxxxx At any rate, one couldn't describe the "leading away" as being quite gentle, and according to my definition Scheuer was treated rough and brutal, which was the cause for his screaming. I only watched this entire scene for a short moment, and then the participants disappeared behind a house, and I did not give any further attention to this matter thereafter.

2.

Hearings continued:

Weilerswist, August 28th, 1945

Upon having been summoned, the chauffeur —, 40 years old, residing in Weilerswist, —, and declared upon questioning about this matter as follows:

It is correct, that on said day in the year 1939 or 1940 (I'm not sure) I brought the Jew Walter Scheuer to the Mayor's Office together with the local police chief. I cannot remember exactly if it was Mr. — or Mr. —.

Said police officer approached me in the "Helle Gäschen," and asked me to help him to take away Scheuer, which I then did.

I'm positively denying to have beaten Scheuer. I was holding on to my bicycle with one hand, and Scheuer with the other hand.

Scheuer was beaten from the back, since he was resisting. I can no longer remember who beat him. The person who saw me, should have seen the other two people as well, and might want to inform on them.

When we arrived at the Mayor's Office Scheuer was put into the cellar by said police officer and by another (according to my knowledge the chief of police —).

I don't know what the above mentioned did

to him in the cellar, since I rode on immediately, in order to do some work on my property.

Thus, if the informant specifies that I hit Scheuer, it is not according to the truth. I'm prepared to affirm the above made statements under oath.

3.

Hearing:

Weilerswist, August 27th, 1945

It appeared —, 45 years old, residing in Weilerswist, — and declared upon being questioned:

I can share the following information on the mistreatment of the Jew Walter Scheuer from Weilerswist by chief police officer — and by — both from Weilerswist:

On said day, in the year 1939 or 1940, the above named police officer and — passed by Gräberstrasse. They held on roughly to Walter Scheuer who was between them, and whom they had arrested earlier, and they were hitting his face with their fists, whereas Walter Scheuer's nose was bleeding. Every time when Scheuer was trying to defend himself, both of them started beating on him again. This continued until I lost sight of said persons. Scheuer's father had already been hauled off earlier, or he left, according to my knowledge to Cologne.

I'm asking that — be interviewed, and possibly be held accountable.

4.

C o p y

-.-.-.-.-.-.

Hearings continued:

Weilerwist, August 29th, 1945

There appeared the electrician —, 43 years old, residing in Weilerswist, — and declared upon questioning about the matter as follows:

On said day I was at home and working in the yard, in what was the year 1940 according to my opinion.

Towards afternoon I suddenly heard screams in the street, thereafter I ran to the front door and saw how the chief of police — was "dragging" the Jew Walter Scheuer up the road to the Mayor's Office.

— had tied Scheuer's hands with a rope, and held the rope in both hands, wherewith he pulled Scheuer along behind him with both of his hands. Scheuer couldn't possibly have resisted, since both of his hands were bound. He was bleeding heavily and was laying on the ground when I saw him, and he refused to come along. Weck then dragged him along the ground and — continually kept kicking Scheuer.

— did not have, ó as he is claiming, ó a bicycle in one hand, but was on foot and was holding the rope in both hands, as stated above.

I called the police chief — to task, whereupon he wanted to oblige me to haul Scheuer off to the Mayor's Office, which I naturally refused.

Thereafter I did not pursue the matter any further. To be sure, I went to see the — family in Weilerswist, or rather his wife, who lives in Scheuer's house at Hauptstrasse, and took her to task because of this, whereupon she answered:

"Scheuer did not want to leave, and tore the range out, whereupon I called chief police officer — on the telephone in order to forcibly remove him."

Further she said, that — stood at the corner and — challenged him to transport the — off, which Weck did voluntarily.

As I heard later, the truth was that Scheuer held on to Mrs. —'s range when they wanted to throw him out of the house, and he should never have been treated that way.

Translation of Jeannette's Birth Certificate

E1.

Birth Certificate

(Registrar's Office C o l o g n e - Nippes__________Nr. 544___)

____________________ Jeannette Marx ____________________

was born on 4 June 1921 ______________________________

in C o l o g n e -Nippes __________________________________

religion, and announced that a female **child was**

Father: Friedrich Salomon Marx, cattle dealer _____

____

Mother: Marianna Seligmann __________________

____

Amendment of Record __ This child, Jeannette Marx

carries the added given name "Sara" based on the ordinance of

17 August 1938 ____

____

____

C o l o g n e -Nippes, ______ 7 January _____1939.

____

seal **The Registrar**

__________________________**Substitute** __*signature* ___ ______

Fees, *-60* RM

No. *279* fee-ord.[46]

English translation of Kindertransport list[47]

1 suitcase
5 shirts
5 pants & 1 over-pants
2 dress pants
5 trimmings
4 pajamas
30 handkerchiefs
3 blouses for skiing
3 polo-shirts
4 laundry-dresses
3 colored aprons
1 gabardine pouch
1 colored coat
1 bolero dress
1 small bolero jacket
1 skirt with blouse
1 hand-warmer (mink)
1 pant skirt & jacket
1 woolen coat-dress
10 pairs of stockings
5 pairs of dress socks
4 ties & 4 shawls
1 handkerchief-holder, 1 theater -purse
1 camera & 1 silver handheld mirror & brush
1 set of flatware & 2 silver spoons & 2 silver coffee spoons
1 photo-album
2 pairs of gloves
1 black doll
2 coral necklaces, 2 bracelets, 1 silver & 1 gold
1 gold medallion, a gold brooch
1 alarm clock, chrome plated
2 bottles of cologne, 2 bottles of anise drops
2 photo-portraits
1 little silhouette picture
1 Bayer-handicraft book
1 book as reading material for the trip
1 French dictionary

1 small English language book
1 Poesie-album
Schoolbooks & report cards
1 magazine with cut-away drawings
1 Vobach-pattern
2 atlas
Diverse books:
Martin Buber – The Legend of the Baalshem
Jacob Prinz – Jewish History
Goethe – Faust
Ibsen – Peer Gynt, a.o.
3 bed-linens 1 small sewing basket
4 tablecloths
1 pair of overshoes 1 sewing machine
4 pairs of shoes
1 fur cap

Entry for Jeannette Marx
To the Foreign Exchange Office Köln-Nippes
Wilhelmstr. 55 [48]

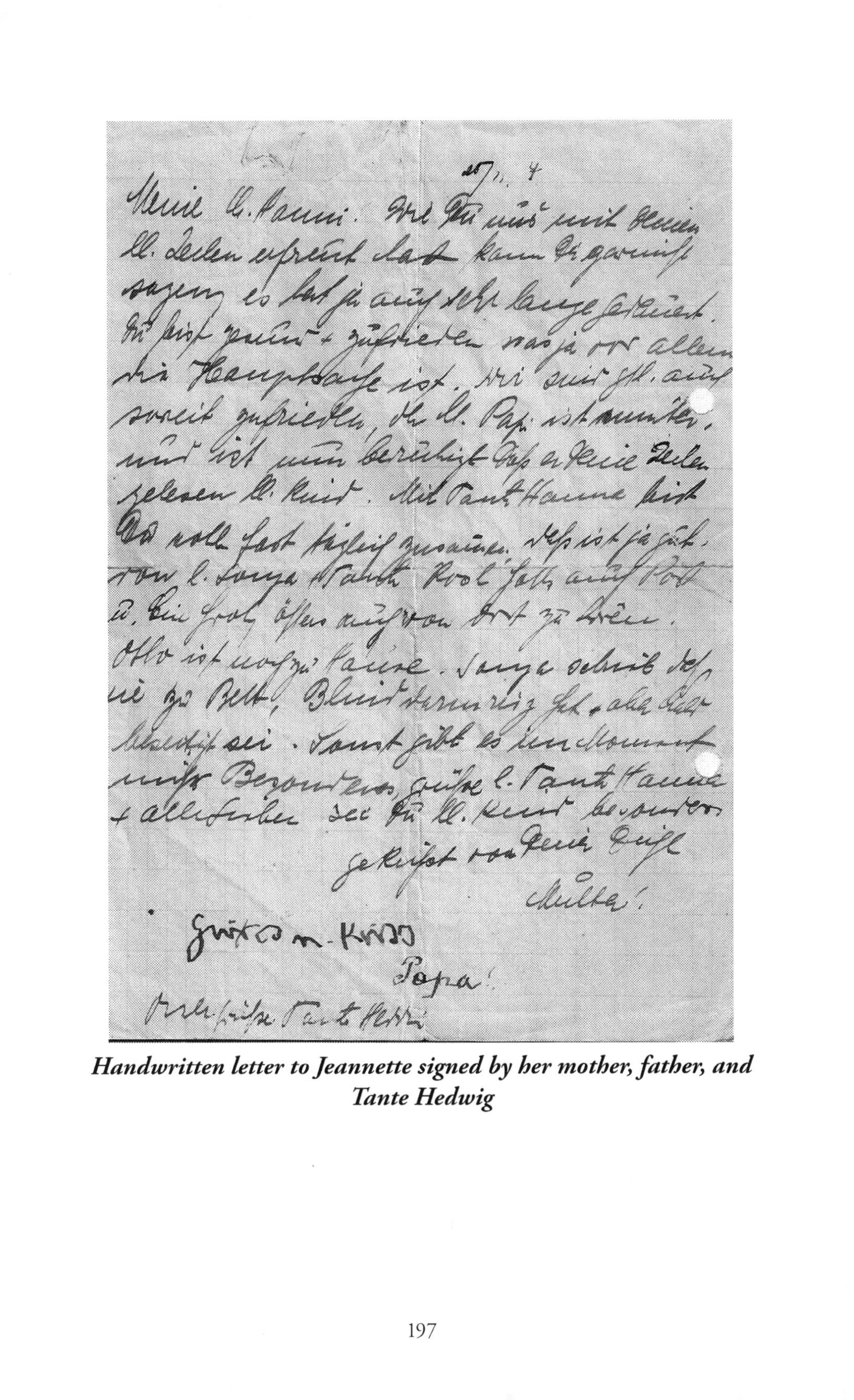

Handwritten letter to Jeannette signed by her mother, father, and Tante Hedwig

LONDON COUNTY COUNCIL

AUXILIARY AMBULANCE SERVICE

THIS IS TO CERTIFY THAT

J. MARX

HAS RECEIVED A COURSE OF TRAINING IN AID RAID PRECAUTIONS AND HAS PASSED AN EXAMINATION IN THE THEORY AND PRACTICE OF THE FOLLOWING SUBJECTS–

(a) GENERAL ORGANISATION OF CIVIL DEFENCE
(b) ANTI-GAS PRECAUTIONS
(c) ELEMENTARY PROTECTION AGAINST HIGH EXPLOSIVE BOMBS
(d) INCENDIARY BOMB CONTROL
(e) USE OF FIRE EQUIPMENT

W. Allen Daley

MEDICAL OFFICER OF HEALTH

(O.18530)

London Auxiliary Ambulance Service Certificate of Training

Rare World War II London Auxiliary Ambulance Service Postcard by artist "SAX."

LONDON COUNTY COUNCIL
THE COUNTY HALL, WESTMINSTER BRIDGE, S.E.1

December, 1945

Dear Madam,

The Council's services in war-time - Staff.

The London County Council, at its meeting on 23rd October, 1945, had before it a report of its Civil Defence and General Purposes Committee reviewing the work of its staff in the civil defence and other services during the six years of war. After considering this report, the Council, as recommended therein, passed a resolution as follows:-

> That the Council places on record its high appreciation of the devotion to duty of all its staff, whether past or present, full-time or part-time, permanent or temporary, paid or unpaid, who, during the six years of the Second World War, 1939-1945, have performed such splendid work, often at great personal sacrifice and risk, both in the civil defence and kindred services administered by the Council and also in the Council's own normal services which have had to be maintained despite all circumstances of war; and that the foregoing report and this resolution be brought to the notice of all individuals concerned in so far as this is possible.

I have great pleasure in communicating the resolution and sending a copy of the report to you as a former member of the London Auxiliary Ambulance Service.

Yours faithfully,

Eric Salmon

Clerk of the Council.

(7552)

Letter of Recognition

<u>C o p y.</u>

Chief District Police Office C o l o g n e, 29 Sept. 40

<u>II J 50/52 M, 110/40.</u> receipt stamp:

27 SEP 1940,*H*

<u>Regarding:</u> Loss of German Citizenship

German Citizenship was lost by:

.... *Marx, Arthur*...............................

born <u>on</u> ... *22 Feb. 1900* in *Weilerwist* ....

last living in .. **Cologne**, ... Schenkendorfstr. 18 ....

<u>due to denaturalization.</u>

Announcement of the RMdI. dated *25 May 1938* published in No.

...*122*.... of the German Empireís and Prussian State Gazette dated

... *28 May 1938*....

----

25 Sep. 40

Chief District Police Office C o l o g n e, ...194...

<u>- II J 50/52 M, 110/40</u>

<u>Original</u>

to the Registrarís Office

<u>in Weilerwist, District of Euskirchen</u>

Your special attention is requested

By proxy:

P…tzsch

1) Note in the Registrarís Books

2) Dated 8 Oct 1940

The Registrar

6219 [49]

Translator's Note/Explanation:

Revocation of naturalization and derecognition of German citizenship of Jewish citizens was legislation added to the German Civil Code on July 14, 1933 (RGB1, I P. 480) by the Nazis. From then on denaturalization of Jews was performed completely legally whenever the authorities chose to implement this law, and Jewish assets could be and were legally seized after Jews had been denaturalized. The Gestapo and Nazi machinery went through an elaborate process of making sure they were adhering to the letter of the Law, collecting files for each single action, and sending out copies to registrarís offices, mayorís offices, police offices, and to banks. It is therefore quite impossible that non-Jewish Germans could not have known what was going on, but the general consensus must have been that the homeland was served better if Jews were denaturalized and sent away, since they now were considered "illegal" and a menace to the German people. In the process of denaturalization their assets could also be legally confiscated, but that was just a "natural by-product" of no longer having citizenship rights in the country. The public did not speak up against confiscation and public auctions of Jewish property (after all, the actual process was according to the "laws of the homeland," added to the Civil Code by Hitlerís government). The majority believed the propaganda that Germany would be better off without Jews, and many others were afraid to speak up — and once again, the process was sanctioned civil laws added on by the new president of the country!

Add. Note: Weilerswist was spelled "Weilerwist" without and s in these documents

Testimony of SA Destruction of Terranova Factory

Hearing:

Weilerswist, September 1st, 1945

It appeared the laborer —Weilerwist, behind —, 42 years old, and explained upon questioning:

Back then I was a laborer at the Terranova-Factory in Weilerswist. On 10 November 1938 my superior at the SA office ordered me to appear at the waiting-room in the Weilerswist Train Station that evening. I was somewhat late, and when I walked up the Bahnhofsstrasse, a brigade of SA men, as well as other people whom I didn't know and had not seen before, came towards me. I joined this troop, which moved along the Grabenweg. Then I saw how some people from this troop began destroying Scheuer's business. But for myself, I did not join in. Later the troop moved on to Moses' business, however I did not come along there for the time being, but watched the proceedings from an entry way. But when I noticed that it was burning at Moses' I went there by myself, and extinguished that small fire by myself. Thereafter I had enough of the entire affair and went home.

I deny to have destroyed anything in the above mentioned matter, or to have stolen anything. [50]

Identification of Apartments.

Although records indicate most of Jeannette's relatives were deported to their deaths towards the end of 1941, any Jewish friends or relatives remaining in Cologne received this notice:

Jewish Religious Federation Cologne, April 7th, 1942

"Associations of Congregations of Cologne"
Roonstrasse 50

To all Jews in Cologne,

I. Regarding: Identification of apartments.

1. Jewish owners of apartments, who are obliged to wear the identification mark, have to identify their apartments.

2. Apartments have to be identified with a Jewish star printed in black on white paper, which is available upon presentation of the police registration at our administrative offices at Roonstrasse 50, 1. Room 3, beginning today between 9 AM and 1 PM. Manufacture of identification marks is not permitted. We will take care of the identification for the cooperative apartments in Müngersdorf, and of group homes[51]. The identification mark has to be attached next to the nameplate, or if there is none, it has

to be glued to the door frame at the entrance on the outside.

3. The apartment has to be identified with only <u>one</u> Jewish star, no matter how many Jews live there who are required to wear the identification.

4. If Jews live in an apartment whose owner is not required to wear identification, they have to affix a separate nameplate with the complete name at the entrance of the apartment, right next to the identification.

5. Persons who live in an apartment whose owner is required to identify the apartment, but who are not required to wear the identification mark, have the right to affix a separate nameplate without the identification.

6. In cases 2, 4, and 5, the nameplates and identification are to be attached in such a manner that it is clear and beyond any doubt to which apartment the identification pertains to.

7. The identification of the apartment has to be undertaken immediately, and has to be completed <u>by 15 April 1942</u> at the latest.

II. Regarding: <u>Use of public transportation within the municipality.</u>

1. Jews are required to wear the identification mark and prohibited to use all public transportation within their municipality without prior written permission of the local police department, effective

May 1, 1942.

2. Written permission to use means of transportation will be issued upon request by the local police department.

a) for Jews in the employment of labor, if as a rule, the distance between the residence and work place is more than one hour on foot, or more than 7 km, for those who were disabled on active service, and for elderly, or otherwise disabled persons, even if the distance between residence and work place is short

b) for school children, if as a rule, the distance between the residence and school is more than one hour on foot, or more than 5 km, for sickly, weak, or frail children even if the distance between residence and school is short

c) for licensed male or female nurses, midwives, and legal advisors.

3. Application for issue of a permit has to be made with the local police department

a) by Jews in the employment of labor through submittal of an attestation issued by the appropriate Federal Employment Office,

b) for school children upon submittal of an attestation by the appropriate school authority.

c) for licensed male and female nurses, midwives, and legal advisors upon submittal of their certificates of registration.

4. These applications are to be submitted on a form that is available at our administrative office, Roonstrasse 50, 1. Floor, Room 3, beginning Friday April 10th, 1942 between 9 AM and 1 PM.

5. Applications for issue of attestation by the Federal Employment Office, or the School Authorities, as well as requests for issue of permits to use means of transportation at the local police department are to be submitted between April 20 and 30, 1942, and on the following days depending on the applicantís name:

A-F on April 20 and 21

G-K on April 22 and 23

L-R on April 24 and 25

S-Z on April 27 and 28, 1942

6. a) The permit of the local police department is issued on a yellow form the size of a postcard, and is valid for one year.

b) The certificate of permission has to be carried whenever a means of transportation is used, together with official photo identification (such as an identity card), and has to be shown upon request.

c) The certificate of permission has to be returned if the preconditions for issue no longer exist or are changed, especially if the apartment or place of employment are changed, and also in all cases after the validity has expired.

Violation of regulations I and II will be prosecuted by the State Police.

III. Regarding: Seizure, confiscation, and forfeiture of property.

It is herewith pointed out that persons who are in possession of forfeited property, or are in debt to someone whose property is forfeited, are required to notify the Chief Financial Exchequer in Berlin within six months after the forfeiture has taken place. The time limit extends from 26 November 1941 to 26 May 1942, based on the announcement in the legal publication of the Reich.

We request timely compliance in fulfilling the obligation of disclosure. Whoever violates this obligation of disclosure, either on purpose or because of negligence, is punishable by three months in jail or with a fine, according to § 7 of the II Ordinance of the Civil Code of the Reich.

IV. Regarding: Bicycles.

We remind of past regulations

in accordance with our circular dated 17 November 1941, and we strongly point out that Jews are prohibited from using bicycles, unless they have received permission by the Secret State Police.[52(1)]

Dr. Julius Israel Bier

Chairperson

Excerpt of Holocaust survivor Rudi Billig's 1946 letter to Jeannette

The Final Solution

Deportation from Lodz Ghetto to Chelmno Extermination Camp

With the Nazi goal of being "Judenrein" or "free" of Jews, in 1939, Jews who did not escape life under the Reich, were now forced into Ghettos. The Jews were placed in these concentration camps right along with incarcerated non-Jewish Germans or Austrians who were there because they were criminals. Murderers, robbers, rapists, and swindlers were allowed free reign in the camps. The Nazis consistently encouraged these inmates to "do what they pleased" to further demoralize, berate, and torture the Jews, and lesser so, the Communists.(2) By 1941, killing Jews, rather than forcing them out, became the accepted mode of operation. Firing squads could not easily be carried out against all of the Jews so the plan to create "extermination centers" was set into place. Jews in the Lodz ghetto were deported to the first extermination camp *Chelmno* in December, 1941.(3) Marianne and several relatives were deported to the Lodz ghetto in October, 1941.

Jewish Virtual Library author Jennifer Rosenberg writes:

> During the High Holy days in the fall of 1941, the news hit—20,000 Jews from other areas of the Reich were being transferred to the

Lodz ghetto. Shock swept throughout the ghetto. How could a ghetto that could not even feed its own population, absorb 20,000 more? The decision had already been made by the Nazi officials and the transports arrived from September through October with approximately one thousand people arriving each day. These newcomers were shocked at the conditions in Lodz. They did not believe that their own fate could ever really mingle with these emaciated people, because the newcomers had never felt hunger. Freshly off the trains, the newcomers had shoes, clothes, and most importantly, reserves of food. The newcomers were dropped into a completely different world, where the inhabitants had lived for two years, watching the hardships grow more acute. Most of these newcomers never adjusted to ghetto life and in the end, boarded the transports to their death with the thought that they must be going somewhere better than the ghetto.(4)

Eleanor H. Ayer, a Holocaust survivor describes life in the Lodz ghetto:

> We started out our existence, I wouldn't call it living, in the Lodz ghetto. Conditions were horrid. We had one room which was our bedroom, our living room, our kitchen, our bathroom. The first few nights Mom and I slept on a mattress on the floor, and mice came in and started running on our faces, so we had to give this up. We shared one bed and Grandma had a cot, and Grandfather had a bed...We all worked...I worked at a brassiere factory. Grandfather worked as a male nurse in one of the factories. Grandma got a job sorting rags and making balls of those colored rags, which were eventually used to make rugs for the Germans. The problem was that the rags were full of lice. So she was bringing the lice home.

Eleanor goes on to explain that the lice carried deadly Typhus and because there was no soap or hot water, people could not keep themselves from contracting it.(5) Lodz was surrounded by barbed wire and wooden fences so escape was virtually impossible. There were about 60,000 residents crammed into each square kilometer of the ghetto and Lodz was the main forced labor camp in existence. Although there were schools, nursing homes, an orphanage, courthouse and a prison, dignity and normalcy were non-existent. Systematic starvation and disease killed many Jews.[6] In late 1941, the Nazis developed a mobile killing van and tested it on Soviet prisoners of war. Because it worked, three more trucks were converted and used in the Ukraine. The goal was now to find a suitable area to operate "discreetly." Chelmno located thirty-five miles northwest of Lodz was where the first death camp was established. The first gassings took place on December 8, 1941 and were carried out using bottled carbon monoxide.[7] Due to continuous deportations to Chelmno, Lodz inhabitants decreased to 70,000 people. In mid June, 1944, as the Soviet Army approached, the remaining Jews were deported to Auschwitz and other concentration camps.[8]

Riga

Riga was the capital of Latvia until the Soviets annexed it. In July, 1941 the Nazis took over and in August a ghetto was established in the city. The Nazis then sealed the ghetto in October 1941 with over 30,000 Jews inside. In November and December over 26,000 Riga Jews were shot to death. 4,000 to 5,000 Jews survived. 20,000 German, Austrian and Jews from other areas were deported to Riga. Most of the remaining German Jews sent to Riga were killed in the Rumbula Forest. Jeannette's friend Rudy Billig recounts, "***We remained at the Ghetto until the end of 1943, and we persevered despite the hunger. Sadly, we were then sent to different concentration camps in the Riga area, and men and women were separated. In these inhuman conditions most everyone perished. Hunger, cold, and mistreatment, were the order of the day. But despite of this I would have succeeded in helping my parents, if only the terrible murders wouldn't have taken place in summer of 44. Everyone over 50 years of age was ordered to appear, and a little bit later everyone older than 30. Among them were my dear parents, and many acquaintances.***" Several hundred Jews in Riga organized resistance activities against the Nazis. Small groups tried to escape and join partisans in the surrounding forests. German police found a small group of underground members outside the ghetto. The Nazis apprehended and killed over 100 people from the ghetto and executed practically all Jewish policemen. According to Rudy's letter, Jeannette's cousin Ine participated in the resistance: "***Your cousin Ine, as well as Otto Seligmann and his mother, were among us as well. (Otto died at the Riga Ghetto from a disease, his***

mother later on at the military hospital, and Ine was present in one of the usual actions at the end of 1943)"

In 1943, some Jews from Riga were deported to Kaiserwald concentration camp and to Kaiserwald sub camps. Riga was destroyed in 1943 and the remaining Jews were sent to Kaiserwald. In 1944 the Nazis forced prisoners to reopen mass graves in the Rumbula forest and burn their bodies. Once finished, they killed these Jewish prisoners. In 1944 Germans killed thousands more Jews in Kaiserwald. The survivors were sent to Stutthof concentration camp.[9]

" Oskar and I were sent by ship to Stutthoff, close to Danzig, and later to Buchenwald, and then to Zeitz in Thuringia."

Buchenwald

The following account is an excerpt taken from a 1945 New York Times newspaper article: ***NAZI DEATH FACTORY SHOCKS GERMANS ON A FORCED TOUR***

The New York Times, Wednesday, April 18, 1945 – Gene Currivan

> Buchenwald, Germany, April 16 (Delayed) – German civilians-1,200 of them-were brought from the neighboring city of Weimar today to see for themselves the horror, brutality and human indecency perpetrated against their "neighbors" at the infamous Buchenwald concentration camp. They saw sights that brought tears to their eyes, and scores of them, including German nurses, just fainted away. They saw more than 20,000 nondescript prisoners, many of them barely living, who were all that remained of the normal complement of 80,000. The Germans were able to evacuate the others before we overran the place on April 10...This Government-controlled camp was considered second only to that at Dachau, near Munich, as the world's worst atrocity center. It had its gallows, torture rooms, dissection rooms, modern crematoria, laboratories where fiendish experiments were made on living human beings and its sections where people were systematically starved to death. This correspondent made a tour of the camp today and saw everything herein described...[10]

Theresienstadt

When Rudi arrived in Theresienstadt, the ghetto "experienced it's final shock when the Germans brought thousands of prisoners who were evacuated from concentration camps. A new outbreak of epidemic sicknesses occurred as a result. On May 3rd, the Nazis handed Theresienstadt over to a Red Cross representative and the last Jew left on August 17th, 1945.(11)

"Shortly before the Americans arrived we were transported eastwards again, the destination unknown. Escape was unthinkable, besides that we didn't know if the news were authentic. Sadly my brother lost his life in a bombing raid, while I, together with a few others, was liberated in Theresienstadt on May 6 by the Red Army, following a 2 week odyssey through Czechoslovakia. After I had also successfully survived spotted fever we remained in Theresienstadt for a while, where we recovered rather quickly."

Auschwitz

As stated previously, Lodz ghetto inhabitants who remained alive in 1944, were deported to Auschwitz and other camps as the Soviet Army approached. Lodz registry records list a date of death for Julius Freund but not for Marianne Marx. Conflicting records and accounts make it difficult to know for certain whether Marianne perished in Lodz or if she was transported at some point to another location. Rudi's account to Jeannette indicates he saw Marianne in Theresienstadt. Jeannette believes that from there she was sent to Auschwitz where she perished. It is certain that Marianne was not alive by the time the United States and Soviet Armies arrived.

The majority of Jews brought to Auschwitz had no time to acclimate themselves to their new environment. Auschwitz served as a mere "exit point" through the gas chamber then to the crematorium. Because of this, even though the Nazis kept very good records, Jews who ultimately perished here were never registered. Auschwitz is, in all probability, the largest cemetery in the world.(12)

Corrected copy of Marianne's Birth Certificate after the Defeat of the Nazi Regime:

Birth Certificates of 111207

A.

Nr. *579*

Nippes, **on** *13 July* **188***9*

Today appeared before the undersigned registrar in person, *the*

___

the merchant Joseph Seligmann ___

residing in *Nippes, Neußerstraße N. 82* ___

of the *Israelite* **religion, and announced that a** *female* **child was**

born to *Jeannette Seligmann, née Kahn, his married spouse* ___

of the *Israelite* **religion** ___

residing *with him* ___

in *Nippes, in his apartment* ___

on *July seventh* **of the year thousand eight hundred eighty** *nine*

in the morning **at** *five* **o'clock** ___

___

who received the given name ___

___ *Marianna* ___

___

Read, approved, and *undersigned*

___ *Seligmann* ___

___

The Registrar

______________________________*Tissen*_________________________

Cologne *Nippes* **This remark in margin dated**

on *7 December 1938 7 December 1938*

This child pertaining to the added

Marianna Seligmann **given name**

based on the ordinance *Sara*

of 17 August 1938 carries is herewith erased

the added given name according to § 6 A ....

Sara **ZJA. Hbg. from 6 Feb. 48.**

The Registrar Cologne, *28 October 1950*

Thierk...tter **The Substitute Registrar**

Translation of corrected copy of Salomon's Birth Certificate after the Defeat of the Nazi Regime:

Nr. *61*

Weilerswist **on** *27 July* **188***8*

Today appeared before the undersigned registrar in person, *the*

the merchant Michael Marx

residing in *Weilerswist*

of the *Israelite* **religion, and announced that a** *male* **child was born to** *Fannÿ Marx, née Nussbaum, his married spouse, without profession*

of the *Israelite* **religion**

residing *with him*

in *Weilerswist in his apartment*

on *July twenty third* **of the year thousand eight hundred eighty** *eight*

in the afternoon **at** *eleven* **o'clock**

who had received the given names

Friedrich Salomon

Read, approved, and *undersigned*

Michael Marx

The Registrar

substituting Opheider

Translation of corrected copy of Salomon's Birth Certificate after the Defeat of the Nazi Regime:

Nr. *61*

Weilerswist **on** *27 July* **188***8*

Today appeared before the undersigned registrar in person, *the*

___

the merchant Michael Marx ___

residing in *Weilerswist* ___

of the *Israelite* **religion, and announced that a** *male* **child was born to** *Fannÿ Marx, née Nussbaum, his married spouse, without profession* ___

of the *Israelite* **religion** ___

residing *with him* ___

in *Weilerswist in his apartment* ___

on *July twenty third* **of the year thousand eight hundred eighty** *eight*

in the afternoon **at** *eleven* **o'clock**

___

___

who had received the given names

___

___ *Friedrich Salomon* ___

Read, approved, and *undersigned*

____________________ *Michael Marx* ____________________

The Registrar

____________________*substituting Opheider* ____________________

Died on *19. March 1941* **in** *Köln-Ehrenfeld*

Reg. *Köln-Ehrenfeld* **No** *286*

Weilerswist, on *26 March 1939,*
based § 2 of ordinance 2 pertaining
to implementation of the Law on
name changes of 17 August 1938,
the one mentioned in opposite record,
Friedrich Salomon Marx, has
adopted the additional given name
Israel, based on declaration dated
2 January 1939, effective on
1 January 1939

the Registrar

This remark in margin dated
26 March 1939 **pertaining to**
the added given name *Israel*
is herewith erased according to § 6 Par. 1
of the Ordinance of the Chief Justice ..
Hamburg dated 16 Feb. 1948

Weilerswist, *4 January 1951*

The Substitute Registrar

Stolpersteine Memorial

Artist Gunter Demnig works out of his studio in Cologne, Germany creating "stumbling stones" to represent and honor the memories of the thousands of individuals who were killed in the Holocaust. Demnig's art was inspired in the early 90's when he traced the route used by gypsies out of Cologne during Nazi deportations. A woman commented to him that she was unaware gypsies once lived in her current neighborhood during the Nazi regime. Demnig realized Holocaust victims were known mostly in an abstract way; in numbers rather than individual names. He decided to create a brass stone for each of them and install them in front of their last homes. In this way, Demnig says, "the name is given back." Although there is a monument in Berlin dedicated to Holocaust victims, "the monument in Berlin is abstract and centrally located," says Deming, who is 60. "But if the stone is in front of your house, you're confronted. People start talking. To think about six million victims is abstract, but to think about a murdered family is concrete." The stumbling stones remind present day Germans that these were people who once lived in their house or apartment.(13)

Acknowledgments

From the beginning, many family members, friends, and acquaintances expressed their support and encouragement as I endeavored to tell the life story of Shoah survivor Jeannette Grunfeld Marx. Special thanks to Jeannette for your patience as I gathered facts and details from our phone interviews and during our visits together. Your charming sense of humor and kindness has made this project every bit worthwhile. Of course, the friendship I have gained in getting to know you is the true gift that has come from this experience.

Thank you to my husband, Arturo, for your patience and continued support. You helped so much in every way, especially by entertaining our little ones while I hammered away at the keyboard. To my mother, who was the "biggest fan" of this story and couldn't wait to be the first one to read it. Thank you Dr. Arturo Aguayo for your practical suggestions and for your willingness to be the very first editor of the *rough* manuscript. Mr. Harold Falk, I extend my thanks to you for taking the time to read and comment on the manuscript as well.

Mr. Kurt Florman, your editing skills on the final draft were invaluable and I truly appreciated the constructive feedback and support that you provided.

Tausend Dank! to Dr. Esther Bauer for translating original hand-written letters and documents from German to English. Your work is meticulous and you were kind enough to answer all of my questions regarding Jewish history and to provide excellent tips and suggestions throughout this process.

German artist Gunter Demnig and Uta Franke, Danke vielmals! for allowing me to use photographs of your *stolpersteine* memorial stones.

When Jeannette saw the photographs of each family member's stone she was deeply moved and stated, "I didn't know about these before. I think that's wonderful!"

Halina Birenbaum, your poetry regarding the Shoah is so eloquent and meaningful, especially because you lived it. Thank you for giving me permission to include your poems in this biography.

Dr. Barbara Becker-Jákli of Stadt Köln - Der Oberbürgermeister NS-Dokumentationszentrum. Thanks to you for permitting the use of documents and photographs for Jeannette's story. My gratitude is given to Yad Vashem and the United States Holocaust Memorial Museum for their vast archival collections and their willingness to share this information with the rest of us.

Herr Peter Kraut, I cannot thank you enough for all of the time you dedicated researching the Marx family archives in Klein Vernich/ Weilerswist. Your contributions are priceless and this project is made complete due to all of the new information you uncovered in regard to this family. Herr Fritz Giese, thank you for the photographs you personally took and provided to me. Finally, thank you, my sons Joshua and Jacob and my princess, Bella, for letting mommy work on the computer, "just a couple of more minutes!"

Bibliography

Quote by Aharon Appelfeld: Applewhite, Ashton, et.al., And I Quote. St. Martin's Press: New York, 1992. pg. 437

Chapter 1

1. An inscription found on the walls of a cellar in Cologne Germany. The poem was believed to be written by Jews in hiding from the Nazis.

2. Gay, Ruth. The Jews of Germany, A Historical Portrait. Connecticut: Yale University Press. 1992. pg. 4

3. Elon, Amos. The Pity of it All: A History of Jews in Germany, 1743-1933 . Henry Holt and Co. LLC: New York. 2002. pg. 21

4. Gidal, Nachum T. Jews in Germany: From the Roman Times to the Weimar Republic. Konemann Verslagsgesellschaft mbH: Cologne. 1998. pg. 10

5. Carroll, James. Constantine's Sword. Houghton Mifflin: New York, 2001 pg. 250

6. Magnus, Shulamit S. Jewish Emancipation in a Germany City; Cologne, 1798–1871. California: Stanford University Press. 1997. pg. 17

7. Blumenthal, Michael W. The Invisible Wall. Counterpoint: Washington, D.C., 1998. pg. 5

8. Ibid. 1998. pg. 6

9. "Gemeinde Weilerswist" Weilerswist Database. [http://www.weilerswist.de] Accessed 01/08/08

10. Peters, Dieter. Land Between Rhine and Maas. Kleve: Germany, 1993.

11. Ibid.

12. Gidal, Nachum T. Jews in Germany: From the Roman Times to the Weimar Republic. Konemann Verslagsgesellschaft mbH: Cologne. 1998. pg. 168

13. Ibid. pg. 312

14. Arthur, Max. The Faces of World War I. Octopus Publishing Group: London. 2007. pg. 122

15. Arthur, Max. The Faces of World War I. Octopus Publishing Group: London. 2007. pg. 57

16. Gidal, Nachum T. Jews in Germany: From the Roman Times to the Weimar Republic. Konemann Verslagsgesellschaft mbH: Cologne. 1998. pg. 318

17. Arthur, Max. The Faces of World War I. Octopus Publishing Group: London. 2007. pg. 240

18. Duffy, Michael. "Feature Articles: Military Casualties of World War One." First World War Database. [http://www.firstworldwar.com/features/casualties.html] Accessed 01/08/08

19. Gavin, Philip. "Hitler in World War One. " History Place Database. [http://www.historyplace.com/worldwar2/riseofhitler/warone.html] Accessed 01/08/08

20. Gidal, Nachum T. Jews in Germany: From the Roman Times to the Weimar Republic. Konemann Verslagsgesellschaft mbH: Cologne. 1998. pg. 323

Chapter 2

1. "A Smashing Engagement." Ohr Somayach International Database. [http://ohr.edu/ask_db/ask_main.php/2632/Q1/] Accessed 09/19/07

2. Kaufman, Michael. "After the Wedding Ceremony." My Jewish Learning Database. [http://www.myjewishlearning.com/lifecycle/Marriage/LiturgyRitualCustom.html] Accessed 05/21/08

Chapter 4

1. "What is a Cohen?" The Center for Kohanim Database. [http://www.cohen –levi.org/the_cohens_heritage/what_is_a_cohen.html] Accessed 09/12/07

2. Reichman, Ruth. "K…lner Karneval" [http://www.serve.com/shea/germusa/kolner.html] Accessed 11/25/07

Chapter 6

1. Schulte, Klaus H. Dokumentation zur Geschichte der Juden am linken Rheinufur. Duesseldorf: Verlag L. Schwann, 1972.

2. Ibid.

3. "Rise of Hitler." MindQuest Educational Database: [http://library.thinkquest.org/26742/hitler.html]-Accessed 08/14/07.

4. Gavin, Philip. "Germans Elect Nazis." The History Place Database. [http://www.historyplace.com/worldwar2/riseofhitler/elect.html] Accessed 08/14/07

5. Fulbrook, Mary.,ed. German History Since 1800 . New York: Oxford University Press 1997. pp. 320, 322.

6. Gavin, Philip. "The Republic Collapses." The History Place Database. [http://www.historyplace.com/worldwar2/riseofhitler/collapse.html] Accessed 08/14/07

7. Kershaw, Ian. Making Friends With Hitler: Lord Londonberry, The Nazis and the Road to War. New York: Penguin Press. 2004. pg. 26

8. Ibid. pg. 31

9. "Social Democratic Party of Germany." Wikipedia Database. [http://en.wikipedia.org/wiki/Social_Democratic_Party_of_Germany].Accessed 01/08/08

Chapter 7

4. 1. "The Burning of the Reichstag." Shoah Education Database: [http://www.shoaheducation.com/reichstag.html] - Accessed October 11, 2007.

2. Gavin Philip. "The Reichstag Burns." The History Place Database: [http://www.historyplace.com/worldwar2/riseofhitler/burns.html.] Accessed October 11, 2007

3. Holocaust Encyclopedia, "Nazi Terror Begins." United States Holocaust Memorial Museum Database: [http://www.ushmm.org/wlc/article.php?lang=en&ModuleId=10005686] Accessed 02/13/08

4. Cabre, Jaime, et al. "The Enabling Act" - March 23,1933." The IB Holocaust Project Database: [http://cghs.dade.k12.fl.us/holocaust/enabling.html]. Accessed October 11, 2007

5. Craig, Gordan A. Germany, 1866-1945. New York: Oxford University Press. 1999. pg. 632

6. Klemperer, Victor. I Will Bear Witness, Volume 1: A Diary of the Nazi Years. Berlin: Aufbau-Verlag GmbH. 1995. pg. 9

Chapter 8

1. Kaplan, Marion A., Between Dignity and Despair: Jewish Life in Nazi Germany. New York: Oxford University Press. 1998. pg. 26

2. Bartoletti Campbell, Susan Hitler Youth-Growing Up in Hitler's Shadow. New York: Scholastic, Inc. 2005. pp. 38–39

3. Bytwerk, Randall, ed. "German Propaganda Archive." Calvin College Database: [http://www.calvin.edu/academic/cas/gpa/fink.htm] Accessed Sept. 7, 2007

4. Klemperer, Victor. I Will Bear Witness, Volume 1: A Diary of the Nazi Years. Berlin: Aufbau-Verlag GmbH. 1995. pg. 13

5. "Fighting the Fires of Hate" pamphlet United States Holocaust Memorial Museum. Washington , DC.

6. Klemperer, Victor. I Will Bear Witness, Volume 1: A Diary of the Nazi Years. Trans. Martin Chalmers. London. Weidenfeld & Nicolson, 1998. pg. 11

7. Johnson, Eric A. Nazi Terror. New York: Basic Books, 2000. pg. 332

8.` "The Nuremberg Laws." Jewish Virtual Library Database: [http://www.jewishvirtuallibrary.org/jsource/Holocaust/nurlaws.html]. Accessed 01/19/08.

Chapter 9

1. Bartoletti Campbell, Susan Hitler Youth-Growing Up in Hitler's Shadow. NewYork: Scholastic, Inc. 2005. pp. 23–25

2. Ibid. pg. 35

3. Kaplan, Marion A., Between Dignity and Despair: Jewish Life in Nazi Germany. New York: Oxford University Press. 1998. pg. 36

Chapter 10

1. "Jewish German Patriots and Jewish Soldiers Reviled, Disregarded, Rejected." Editrix Database: [http://www.editrixoffice.com/ME_patriots.html] Accessed 01/15/08

2. Friedländer, Saul. Nazi Germany and the Jews Volume I. New York: Harper Collins Publishers. 1977 pg. 16

3. Kaplan, Marion A., Between Dignity and Despair: Jewish Life in Nazi Germany. New York: Oxford University Press. 1998. pg. 148

Chapter 11

1. Holocaust Encyclopedia. "Kristallnacht: A Nationwide Pogrom, November 9-10, 1938." United States Holocaust Memorial Museum Database: [http://www.ushmm.org/wlc/article.php?lang=en&ModuleId=10005201] Accessed 09/08/07

2. Kaplan, Marion A., Between Dignity and Despair: Jewish Life in Nazi Germany. New York: Oxford University Press. 1998. pg. 125

3. "Restored Torah returned to Synagogue," Washington Times Database: [http://washingtontimes.com/apps/pbcs.dll/article?AID=/20071110/FOREIGN/111100029/1003] Accessed 02/22/08

4. "Hearing: Weilerswist, September 1st, 1945." Archive of the Registrar's Office Weilerswist. Courtesy of German historian Peter Kraut

5. Goldhagen, Daniel J. Hitler's Willing Executioners: Ordinary Germans and the Holocaust New York: Knopf, 1996. pg. 102

Chapter 12

1. Transport Association "Brief History." KTA Database: [http://www.kindertransport.org/history.html] Accessed 01/19/08

2. Kaplan, Marion A., Between Dignity and Despair: Jewish Life in Nazi Germany. New York: Oxford University Press. 1998. pg. 117

Chapter 13

1. Kaplan, Marion A., Between Dignity and Despair: Jewish Life in Nazi Germany. New York: Oxford University Press. 1998. pg. 78

Chapter 14

1. Widner, James F. "Britain Goes to War" Radio News Database: [http://www.otr.com/neville.shtml]. Accessed 01/10/08.
2. Ziegler, Philip., London at War 1939–1945. New York: Alfred A. Knopf. 1995. pp. 36–37
3. Ibid. pp. 14–15
4. Ibid. 1995. pg. 29
5. Ibid. pg. 35
6. Kaplan, Marion A., Between Dignity and Despair: Jewish Life in Nazi Germany. New York: Oxford University Press. 1998. pg. 69
7. Ziegler, Philip., London at War 1939–1945. New York: Alfred A. Knopf. 1995. pg. 23
8. "A Report on Visits to Internment Camps for Aliens." Jewish Virtual Library Database: [http://www.jewishvirtuallibrary.org/jsource/Holocaust/chiefrabbi.html]. Accessed Sept 9, 2007

Chapter 15

1. Ziegler, Philip., London at War 1939-1945. New York: Alfred A. Knopf. 1995. pg. 113-114
2. Ibid. pg. 115

3. Ibid. pp. 118–119

4. Raby, Angela. The Forgotten Service-Auxiliary Ambulance Station 39. United Kingdom: Isis Publishing, Ltd. 1999. pg. 60

5. Ibid. pp. 51–52

6. Ibid. pg. 39

7. Ibid. pg. 19

8. Ibid. pg. 161

Chapter 16

1. Raby, Angela. The Forgotten Service-Auxiliary Ambulance Station 39. United Kingdom: Isis Publishing, Ltd. 1999. pg. 30

2. Ibid. pg. 121

3. Ibid.

4. Ibid. pg. xii.

5. Windsor, Joan. "Joan Windsor's WW2 Experiences in Canonbury Road, London." BBC WW2 Database: [http://www.bbc.co.uk/ww2peopleswar/stories/07/a4369007.shtml] Accessed 01/22/07.

6. Klemperer, Victor. I Will Bear Witness, Volume 1: A Diary of the Nazi Years. Trans. Martin Chalmers. London: Weidenfeld & Nicolson, 1998. pg. 196

7. Ziegler, Philip., London at War 1939–1945. New York: Alfred A. Knopf. 1995. pg. 238

8. Turner, Barry Countdown to Victory: The Final European Campaigns of World War II. New York: HarperCollins Publishers, Inc. 2004. pg. 108

9. Brinkley, Douglas, Ed. World War II: The Allied Counter Offensive, 1942-1945. New York: Henry Holt and Company, LLC. 2003 pg. 330

10. Ibid. pg. 331

11. "1945: Germany Signs Unconditional Surrender." BBC News Database: [http://news.bbc.co.uk/onthisday/hi/dates/stories/may/7/newsid_3578000/3578325.stm]. Accessed 01/12/08

12. Salmon, Eric. Letter. London County Council. December, 1945

Chapter 17

1. Billig, Rudi. Personal Letter to Jeannette Grunfeld. Trans. Esther Bauer, PhD.

2. Schulte, Klaus H. Dokumentation zur Geschichte der Juden am linken Rheinufur. Duesseldorf: Verlag L. Schwann, 1972. Provided courtesy of German historian Peter Kraut

Author's Note:

1. De Marco, Donald and Benjamín Wiker. Architects of the Culture of Death. San Francisco: Ignatius Press, 2004. pg. 117

2. Smith, Wesley J. "Killing Babies, Compassionately." The Daily Standard Database: [http://www.weeklystandard.com/Content/Public/Articles/000/000/012/003dncoj.asp] Accessed 10/23/08

3. Lifton, Robert Jay. "German Doctors and the Final Solution." New York Times Database: [http://query.nytimes.com/gst/fullpage.html?sec=health&res=9A0DEED91E39F932A1575AC0A960948260]. Accessed October 23, 2008

4. Ibid. Accessed October 24, 2008

5. "Science as Salvation: Weimar Eugenics, 1919-1933." United States Holocaust Memorial Museum Database: [http://www.ushmm.org/wlc/article.php?lang=en&ModuleId=10007062]. Accessed 10/23/08

6. Lombardo, Paul. "Eugenic Sterilization Laws." Dolan DNA Learning Center Database: [http://www.eugenicsarchive.org/html/eugenics/essay8text.html]. Accessed 10/23/08

7. Sanger, Margaret. The Pivot of Civilization. New York: Brentano's, 1922. pg. 274

8. Sanger, Margaret. Woman and the New Race. New York: Eugenics Publishing Company, 1920. pg. 89

9. De Marco, Donald, Wiker, Benjamin. Architects of the Culture of Death. San Francisco: Ignatius Press, 2004. pg. 116

10. Verhagen, Eduard, M.D., J.D., and Pieter J.J. Sauer, M.D., Ph.D. "The Groningen Protocol-Euthanasia in Severely Ill Newborns." The New England Journal of Medicine Database: [http://content.nejm.org/cgi/content/short/352/10/959] Accessed 10/23/08

11. A. B. Jotkowitz, M.D., and S. Glick. "The Groningen Protocol: Another Perspective." Journal of Medical Ethics Database: [http://jme.bmj.com/cgi/content/abstract/32/3/157] Accessed 10/23/08

12. Singer, Peter. "FAQ- Peter Singer Website." Princeton University Database: [http://www.princeton.edu/~psinger/faq.html] Accessed 10/24/08

13. Shulstein, Moishe. *I Saw a Mountain.* Source: Translated by Beatrice Stadtler and Mindele Wajsman in *From Holocaust to New Life*, edited by Michael Berenbaum (New York: The American Gathering of Jewish Holocaust Survivors, 1985), pg. 121.

14. Nielmoller, Pastor Martin. *First They Came...* Source: Attributed to Pastor Martin Niemoller, as stated in Franklin H. Littell's forward to *Exile in the Fatherland, Martin Niemoller's Letters from Moabit Prison,* edited by Hubert G. Locke (Grand Rapids, Michigan: William B. Eerdman's Publishing Company, 1986), pg. viii.

In Memoriam

1. Dobroszycki, Lucjan. The Chronicle of the Lodz Ghetto, 1941-1944. Connecticut: Yale University Press. 1984. pg. Lviii.

2. Rotbein-Flaum, Shirley. "Lodz Ghetto Deportations and Statistics." JewishGen Database: [http://www.shtetlinks.jewishgen.org/lodz/statistics.html]. Accessed 01/13/08.

Poesie Album — Remembering Who They Were

1. Grunfeld, Jeannette. Poesie Album: Cologne, Germany. Trans. Esther Bauer, PhD

2. Seligmann, Marianne." The Central Database of Shoah Victims' Names: Yad Vashem Database: [http://www.yadvashem.org/wps/portal/IY_HON_Entrance] Accessed 04/05/07

3. "Lodz-Names: A Record of the 240,000 Inhabitants of the Łódź Ghetto." Jewish Gen Database: [http://www.jewishgen.org/databases/poland/lodzghetto.html] 04/05/07

4. Schulte, Klaus H. Dokumentation zur Geschichte der Juden am linken Rheinufur. Duesseldorf: Verlag L. Schwann, 1972.

5. "Scheuer, Walter." The Central Database of Shoah Victims' Names: Yad Vashem Database. [http://www.yadvashem.org/wps/portal/IY_HON_Entrance] Accessed 10/01/2008

6. "Scheuer, Bertha." The Central Database of Shoah Victims' Names: Yad Vashem Database. [http://www.yadvashem.org/wps/portal/IY_HON_Entrance] Accessed 10/01/2008

7. "Seligmann, Paula." The Central Database of Shoah Victims' Names: Yad Vashem Database. [http://www.yadvashem.org/wps/portal/IY_HON_Entrance] Accessed 04/05/07

8. "Seligmann, Otto." NS-Dokumentationszentrum der Stadt Köln Database [http://www.museenkoeln.de/ns-dok/default.a

sp?s=763&tid=323&kontrast=&schrift=&buchstabe=S&id=1135] Accessed 02/15/08

9. "Seligmann, Emilie." The Central Database of Shoah Victims' Names: Yad Vashem Database. [http://www.yadvashem.org/wps/portal/IY_HON_Entrance] Accessed 02/19/08

10. "Freund, Hedwig." The Central Database of Shoah Victims' Names: Yad Vashem Database. [http://www.yadvashem.org/wps/portal/IY_HON_Entrance] Accessed 04/05/07

11. "Freund, Julius." The Central Database of Shoah Victims' Names: Yad Vashem Database. [http://www.yadvashem.org/wps/portal/IY_HON_Entrance] Accessed 04/05/07

Appendix

1. *1942 Notice to Cologne Jews from the Jewish Religious Federation.* Judisches Schicksal in Koln 1918-1945. Historisches Archiv der Stadt Koln NS-Dokumentationszentrum. Trans. Esther Bauer, Ph.D.

2. Edelheit, Abraham J., and Hershel. History of the Holocaust—A Handbook and Dictionary. Colorado: Westview Press, 1994. pg. 68

3. **"Lodz."** Yad Vashem Database: [http://www.yadvashem.org/wps/portal/!ut/p/_s.7_0_A/7_0_S5?New_WCM_Context=http://namescm.yadvashem.org/wps/wcm/connect/Yad+VaShem/Hall+Of+Names/Lexicon/en/Lodz] - Accessed 02/11/08.

4. Rosenberg, Jennifer. "The Lodz Ghetto." Jewish Virtual Library Database: [http://www.jewishvirtuallibrary.org/jsource/Holocaust/lodz.html] Accessed 03/6/08.

5. Ayer, Eleanor H. In The Ghettos: Teens Who Survived the Ghettos of the Holocaust. New York: Rosen Publishing Group. Pgs. 20, 22.

6. Flaum Rotbein, Shirley, et al. "Lodz-Names: A Record of the 240,000 Inhabitants of the Łódź Ghetto." Jewish Gen

Database: [http://www.jewishgen.org/databases/Poland/LodzGhetto.html] Accessed 03/18/08.

7. Breithman, Richard. Chelmno: First Death Camp in Operation. The Architect of Genocide: Himmler and the Final Solution. New York: A. Knopf, 1991, p 202.

8. Flaum Rotbein, Shirley, et al. Lodz-Names: A Record of the 240,000 Inhabitants of the Łódź Ghetto Shirley Rotbein Flaum, et.al. Jewish Gen Database: [http://www.jewishgen.org/databases/Poland/LodzGhetto.html] Accessed 03/18/08.

9. "Riga." Yad Vashem Database: [http://www.yadvashem.org/wps/portal/!ut/p/_s.7_0_A/7_0_S5?New_WCM_Context=http://namescm.yadvashem.org/wps/wcm/connect/Yad+VaShem/Hall+Of+Names/Lexicon/en/Riga] Accessed 02/11/08

10. "Theresienstadt." Yad Vashem Database: [http://www.yadvashem.org/wps/portal/!ut/p/_s.7_0_A/7_0_S5?New_WCM_Context=http://namescm.yadvashem.org/wps/wcm/connect/Yad+VaShem/Hall+Of+Names/Lexicon/en/terezen] Accessed 02/22/08

11. Brinkley, Douglas, Ed. World War II; the Allied Counteroffensive, 1942-1945. New York: Times Books, 2003. pg. 296

12. Edelheit, Abraham J., and Hershel. History of the Holocaust-A Handbook and Dictionary. Colorado: Westview Press, 1994. pg. 69

13. *Stolpersteine*. Demnig, Gunter. [http://www.stolpersteine.com/start.html] Accessed 02/23/08.

Photographic Credits

Cologne Cathedral/Courtesy of Julien Bryan/Courtesy of United States Holocaust Memorial Museum (USHMM).

Glockengasse Synagogue – 1861
Courtesy of Germany Wikipedia – Public Domain

Euskirchen Synagogue
Courtesy of Dokumentation zur Geschichte der Juden am linken Rheinufer seit dem 17. Jahrhundert von Klaus Schulte

Reichstag Fire (Riksdagsbrannen)
Source: National Archives and Records Administration (arcweb.archives.com) Courtesy of Wikipedia

Nieder Mit Juda!
Courtesy of Historisches Archiv der Stadt Koln NS-Dokumentationszentrum

Kristallnacht Jewish Shop Destroyed
Source: National Archives and Records Administration, Courtesy of the United States Holocaust Memorial Museum

Glockengasse Synagogue After Kristallnacht (Synagoge in der Glockengasse)
Source: Cologne Museum (Museenkoeln.de/ns-dok/default)

Jewish Youth's Arrival in England from Kindertransport
Courtesy of USHMM

The Center of Cologne after the first 1,000 Bomber Raid

Courtesy of Wikimedia/U.S. Army Archive

Warning Posted in Front of Cologne Cathedral
Courtesy of Wikimedia/U.S. Army Archive

In Memoriam:

Stolpersteine Photographs
Courtesy of artist Gunter Demnig

Appendix:

Michael Marx "Cohen" Gravestone
Courtesy of Fritz Giese

Lodz Deportation to Chelmno

Courtesy of USHMM

Other Credits:

Translated Marx Family Lineage Records
Translated Michael Marx' Gravestone
Translated Arthur Marx' Loss of German Citizen Document
Translated Testimony of Walter Scheuer Assault
Translated Testimony of SA Destruction of Terranova Factory
Documents researched and provided courtesy of German historian Peter Kraut_
Sources: Weilerswister Heimatblätter Heft 6, Die Einwohnerlisten aus der franz…sischen Zeit „Vernich"edited by Bernd Meyerhoff, Archive at the Registrar's Office Weilerswist, Birth, Marriage, and Death Records. Historian Peter Kraut

Michael Marx Gravestone:
Source: Jewish cemeteries in the Municipality of Weilerswist by Dan Z. Bondy. *In a Past Not Forgotten* by Margarete Fiedler and Helene Kürten. 1988

All translations provided by Esther Bauer, PhD.

All other documents and photographs contained herein were provided courtesy of Jeannette Grunfeld.

(Endnotes)

1 Inscription written by a Jew in hiding. It was found on a cellar wall in Cologne, Germany

2 Refer to Appendix: Marx Family Lineage

3 Source: "Dokumentation zur Geschichte der Juden am linken Rheinufer seit dem 17. Jahrhundert von Klaus Schulte".

4 This Hebrew saying is attributed to the Jewish sage Hillel

5 *Matzah* is the unleavened bread and the *Afikomen* is the largest piece of the Matzah that is broken

6 Name Substitution

7 Name Substitution

8 **Source:** Dieter Peters, Land between Rhine and Maas, Kleve 1993

9 See Appendix for English translation

10 See Appendix for English translation

11 Letters are translated from old, hand-written originals, where words are illegible, an explanation will appear in parenthesis or in the footnotes.

12 Jo is Tante Hanna's nickname

13 See Appendix for copy of original letter in German

14 In the sense of "improve", and of course meant light-heartedly

15 Cousin Ilse may be the actual writer

16 Aunt Hedwig lived in an apartment on the upper floor

17 Last line or possibly a page may be missing from original

18 surname unclear/unsure

19 See Appendix for Theresiendstadt description

20 literally: Zores

21 German word may be misspelled; "Escape" is most likely what was meant.

22 See Appendix to view original hand-written letter

23 See Appendix for Arthur Marx' 1940 "Loss of German Citizenship" Document

24 Refer to the Appendix: Translated Index Card (s) from German Archives re: Marianne Marx

25 **Source:** Dieter Peters, Land between Rhine and Maas, Kleve 1993

26 Refer to the Appendix: *Deportations and Ghettos*

27 Translator notes: This poem was very popular at the time and quoted in many Germany Poetry albums

28 Excerpt taken from "My Father" a poem written by Auschwitz Survivor and novelist, Halina Birkenbaum

29 Index cards provided courtesy of the United States Holocaust Memorial Museum

30 meaning of abbrev. unsure

31 meaning of abbrev. unsure

32 Excerpt taken from "Mother Do You See Me?" a poem written by Auschwitz Survivor and novelist, Halina Birkenbaum

33 See Index regarding Stolpersteine or "Stumbling Stone" Project

34 See Appendix for redacted testimonies from an eyewitness and those accused of the assault

35 See Appendix for Jeannette Marx Family Lineage

36 See Appendix for detailed description of Riga Ghetto

37 Birth, Death, and Marriage Certificates are from the Archive of the Registrar's Office Weilerswist-Courtesy of German historian Peter Kraut

38 Cohen

39 Source: Klaus H. Schulte, Dokumentation zur Geschichte der Juden am linken Niederrhein seit dem 17. Jahrhundert

40 Source: Weilerswister Heimatblätter Heft 6, Die Einwohnerlisten aus der franz…sischen Zeit „Vernich“ edited by Bernd Meyerhoff, Archive at the Registrar's Office Weilerswist, Birth, Marriage, and Death Records.

41 Source: Archive at the Registrar's Office Weilerswist, Birth, Marriage, and Death Records

42 Source: Weilerswister Heimatblätter Heft 6, Die Einwohnerlisten aus der franz…sischen Zeit „Vernich" edited by Bernd Meyerhoff, Archive at the Registrar's Office Weilerswist, Birth, Marriage, and Death Records.

43 See Appendix for SA Testimony of the destruction of the Terra Nova Factory

44 Jeannette's paternal great-great grandfather. Note: Faint view of Cohen hands

45 the word "mentally disabled" is not used, rather "challenged"

46 Translated by Esther Bauer, PhD

47 Items are excerpted from the original List

48 Translated by Esther Bauer, Ph.D.

49 Translated by Esther Bauer, Ph.D.

50 Translated by Esther Bauer, PhD

51 literally: "Heim", which could include nursing homes, orphanages, etc.

52 the Gestapo